Get Physical, SNOOPY!

by Charles M. Schulz

Selected Cartoons from
"I'M NOT YOUR SWEET BABBOO!"
Volume 3

FAWCETT CREST • NEW YORK

A Fawcett Crest Book
Published by Ballantine Books

First published in book form in 1984

 Published in the United States by Ballantine Books, a division of Random House, Inc., New York, and simultaneously in Canada by Random House of Canada Limited, Toronto.

Library of Congress Catalog Card Number: 84-80690

ISBN 0-449-20789-7

This book comprises a portion of I'M NOT YOUR SWEET BABBOO! and is published by arrangement with Holt, Rinehart and Winston

Manufactured in the United States of America

First Ballantine Books Edition: June 1986

10 9 8 7 6 5 4 3 2 1

Get Physical, SNOOPY!

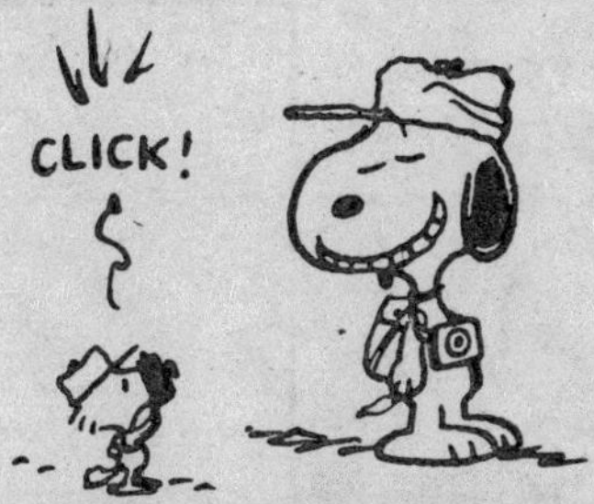
CLICK!

Dear Charles,
Only one more day of camp. Then we can be together again.
Hi, Chuck! Tomorrow we go home. How about me coming over to see you?
Dear Marcie and Patty,
I won't be here when you get home.
I have enlisted in the Navy for two hundred years.
SCHULZ

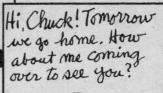

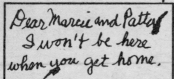

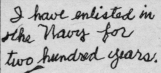

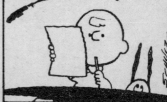

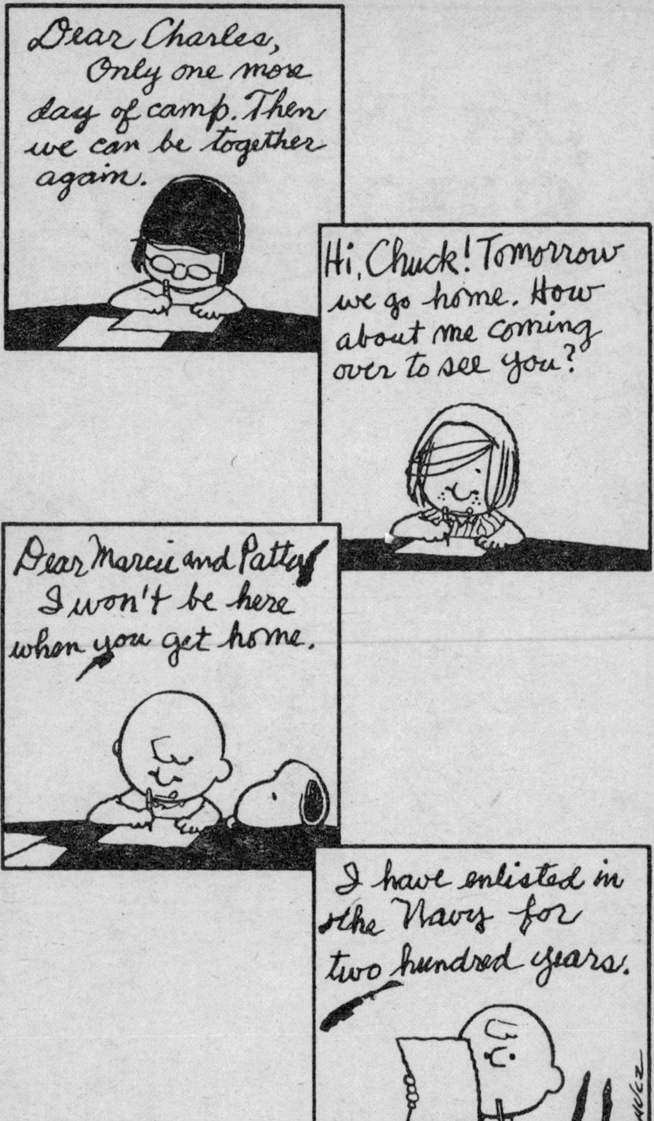

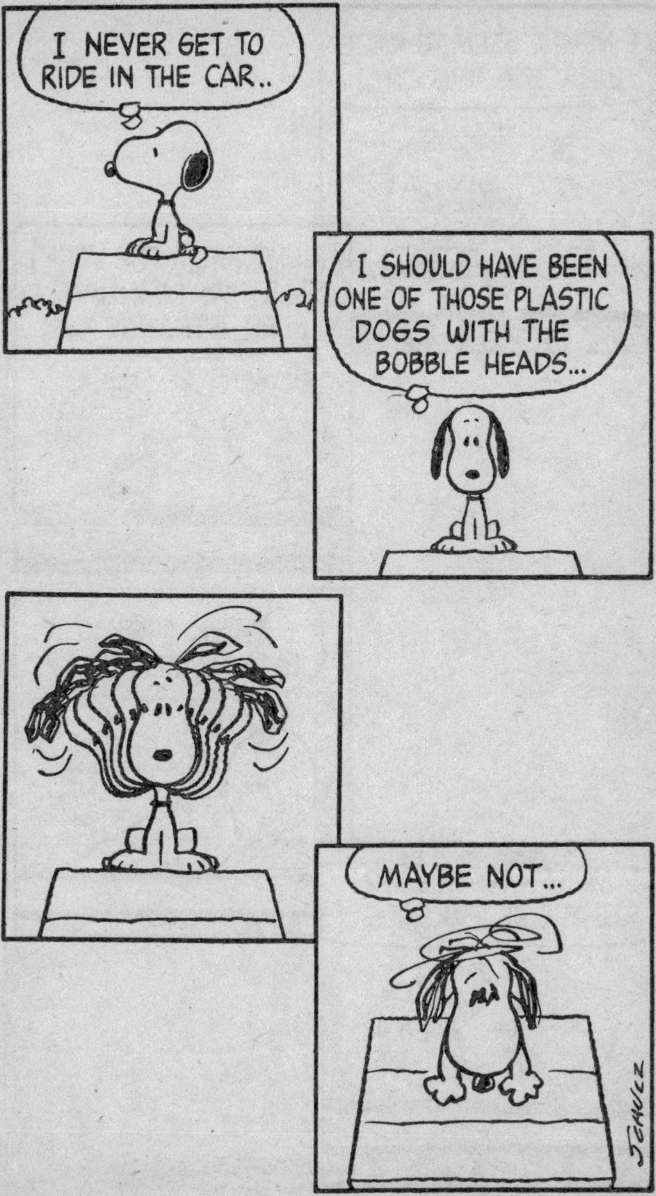
I NEVER GET TO RIDE IN THE CAR..
I SHOULD HAVE BEEN ONE OF THOSE PLASTIC DOGS WITH THE BOBBLE HEADS...
MAYBE NOT...
SCHULZ

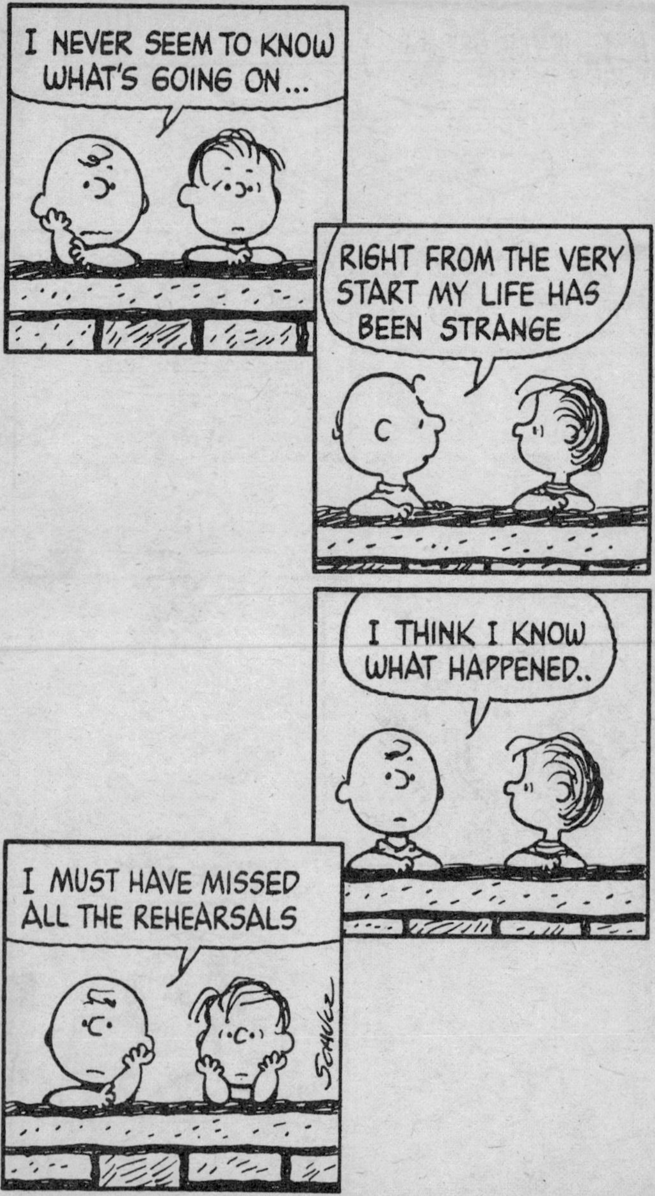
I NEVER SEEM TO KNOW WHAT'S GOING ON...
RIGHT FROM THE VERY START MY LIFE HAS BEEN STRANGE
I THINK I KNOW WHAT HAPPENED..
I MUST HAVE MISSED ALL THE REHEARSALS
SCHULZ

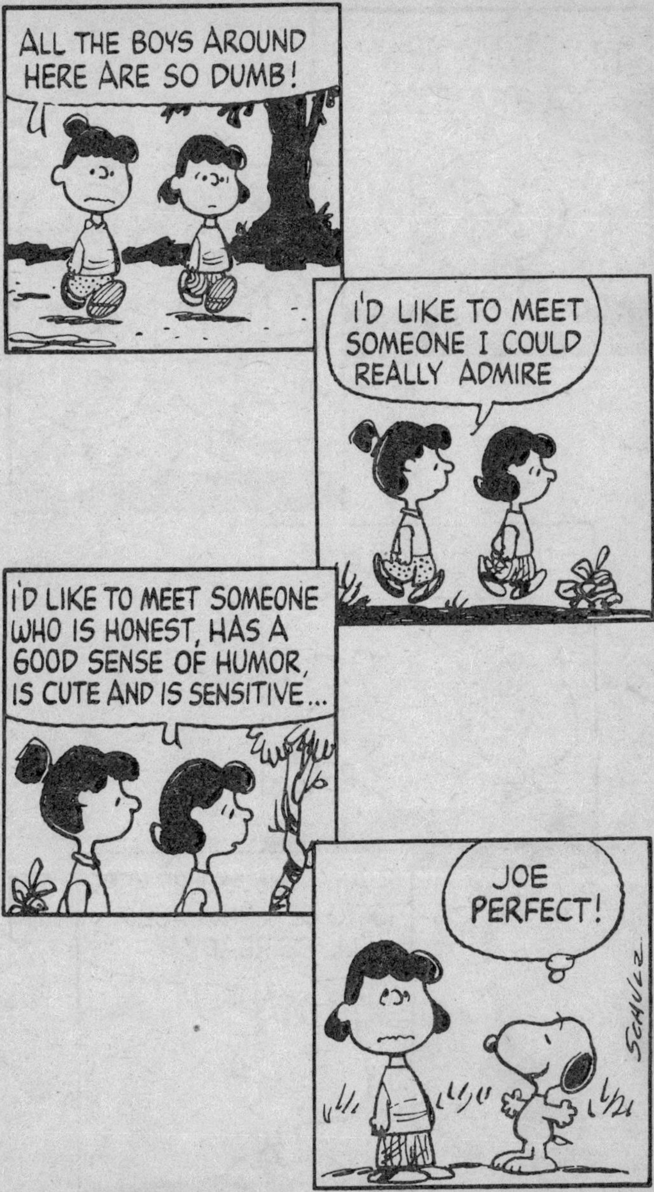
ALL THE BOYS AROUND HERE ARE SO DUMB!
I'D LIKE TO MEET SOMEONE I COULD REALLY ADMIRE
I'D LIKE TO MEET SOMEONE WHO IS HONEST, HAS A GOOD SENSE OF HUMOR, IS CUTE AND IS SENSITIVE...
JOE PERFECT!
SCHULZ

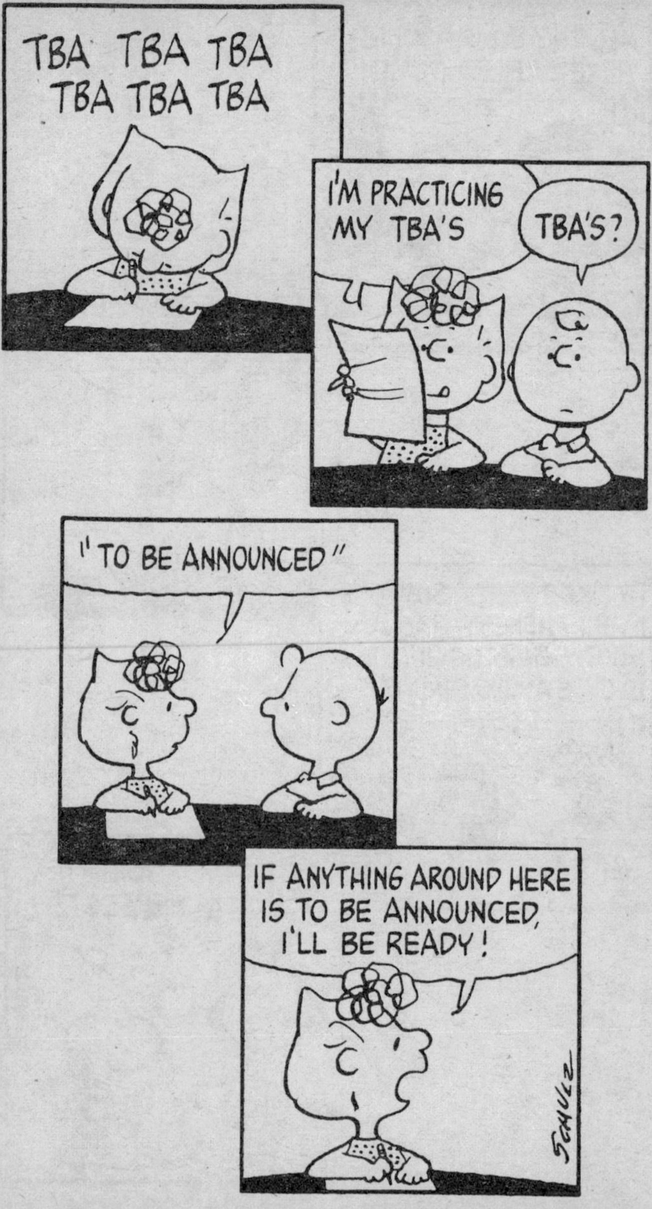
TBA TBA TBA
TBA TBA TBA
I'M PRACTICING MY TBA'S
TBA'S?
"TO BE ANNOUNCED"
IF ANYTHING AROUND HERE IS TO BE ANNOUNCED, I'LL BE READY!
SCHULZ

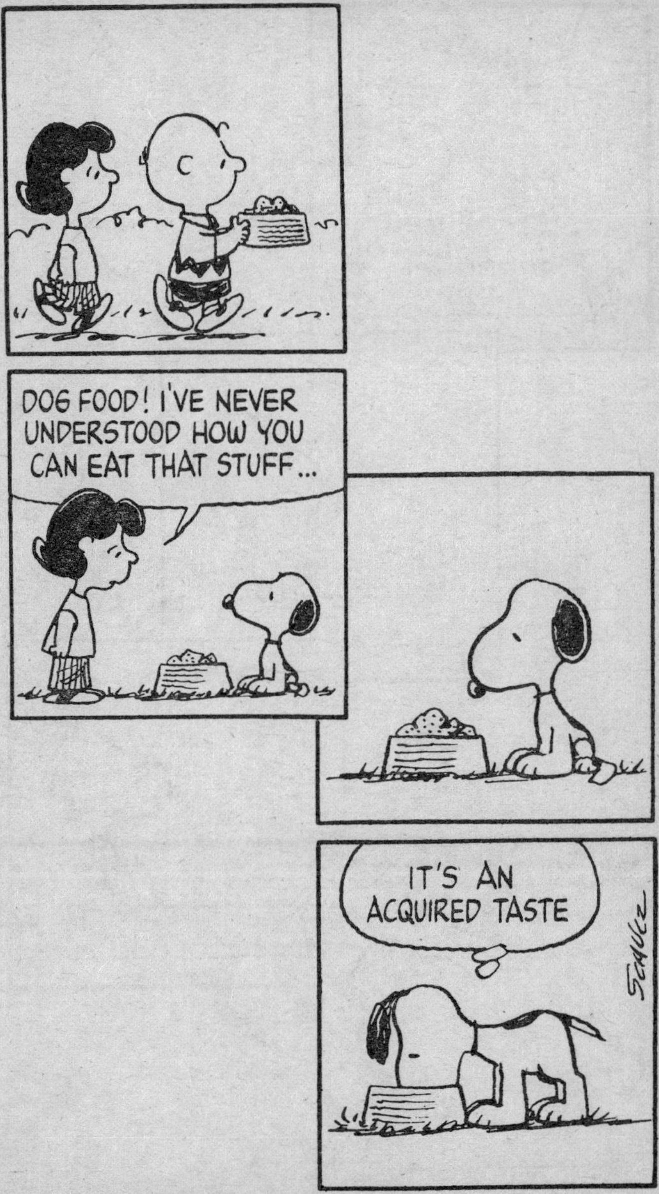
DOG FOOD! I'VE NEVER UNDERSTOOD HOW YOU CAN EAT THAT STUFF...
IT'S AN ACQUIRED TASTE
SCHULZ

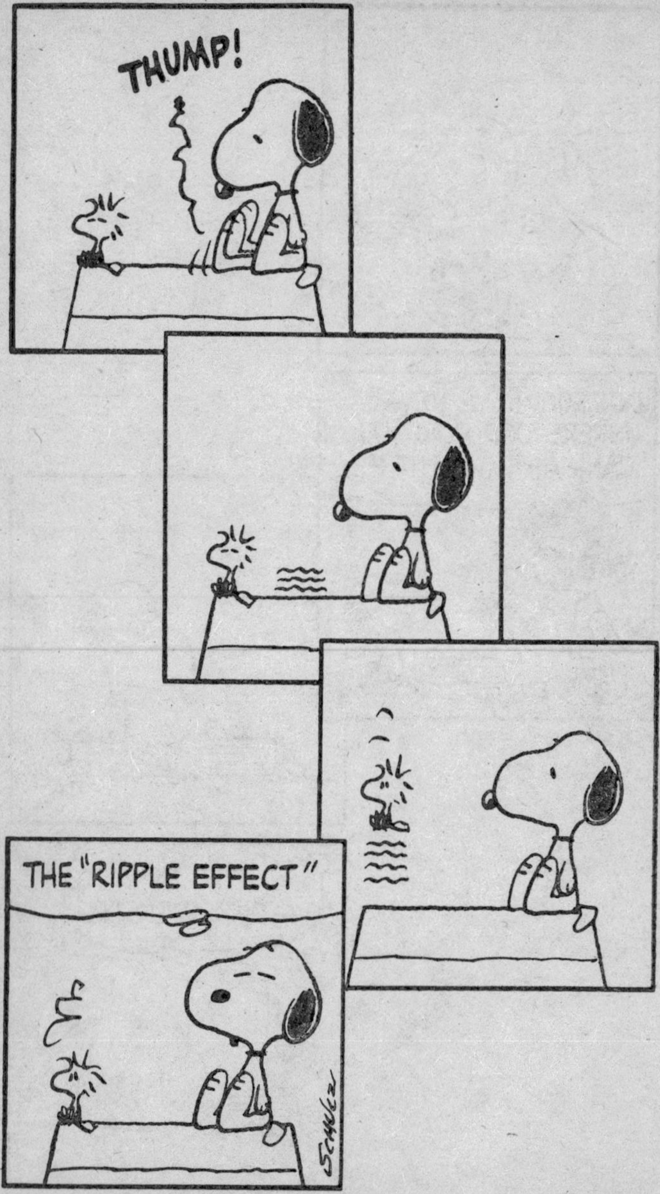
THUMP!
THE "RIPPLE EFFECT"
SCHULZ

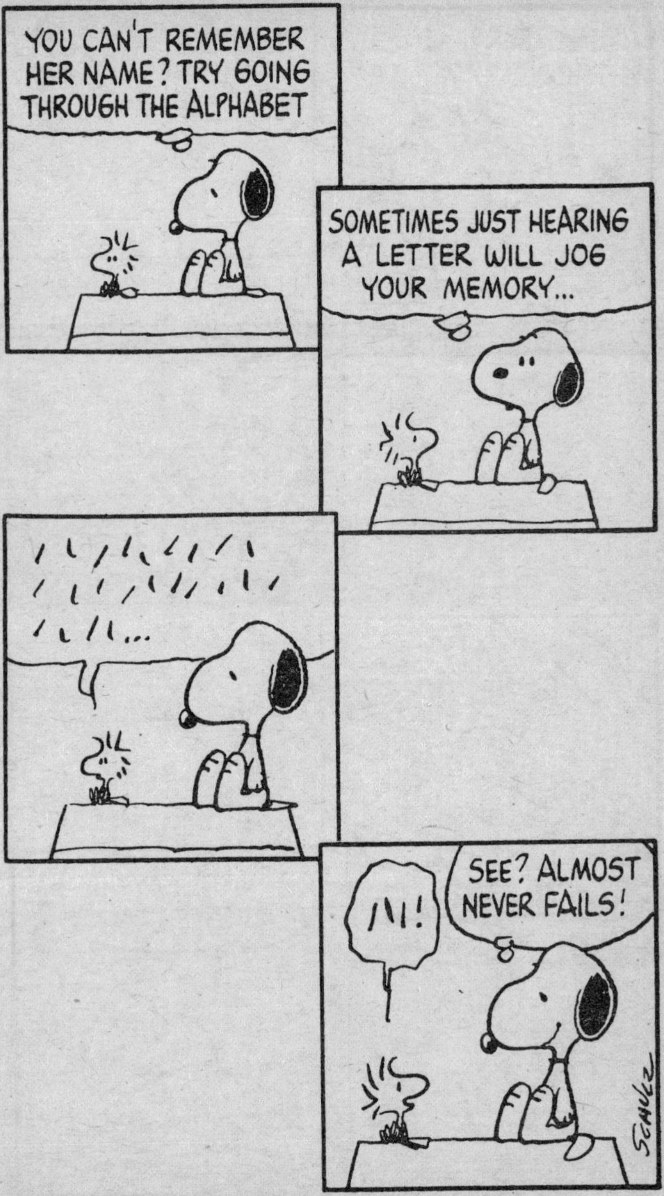
YOU CAN'T REMEMBER HER NAME? TRY GOING THROUGH THE ALPHABET
SOMETIMES JUST HEARING A LETTER WILL JOG YOUR MEMORY...
SEE? ALMOST NEVER FAILS!
SCHULZ

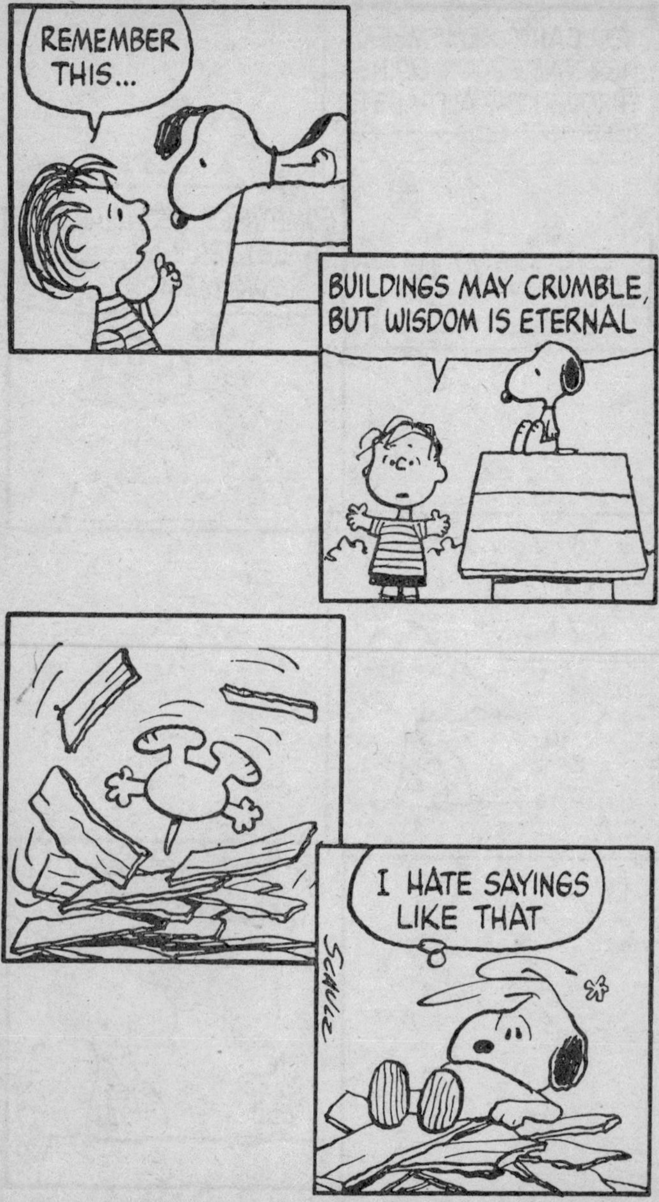
REMEMBER THIS...
BUILDINGS MAY CRUMBLE, BUT WISDOM IS ETERNAL
I HATE SAYINGS LIKE THAT
SCHULZ

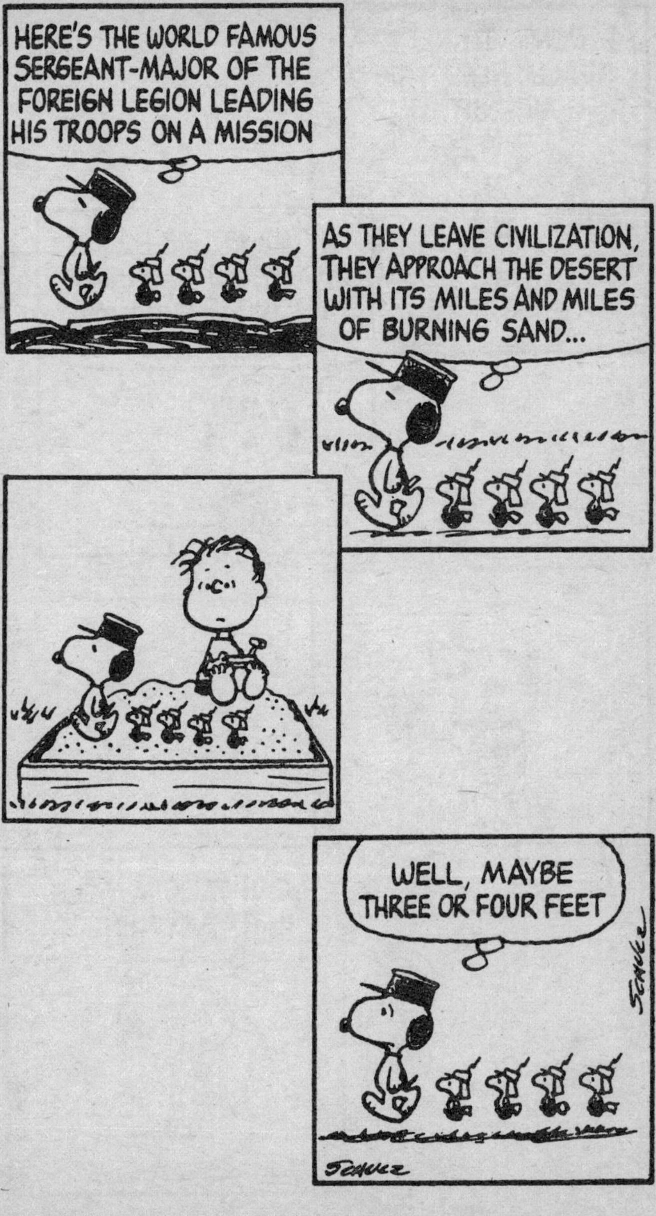
HERE'S THE WORLD FAMOUS SERGEANT-MAJOR OF THE FOREIGN LEGION LEADING HIS TROOPS ON A MISSION
AS THEY LEAVE CIVILIZATION, THEY APPROACH THE DESERT WITH ITS MILES AND MILES OF BURNING SAND...
WELL, MAYBE THREE OR FOUR FEET
SCHULZ

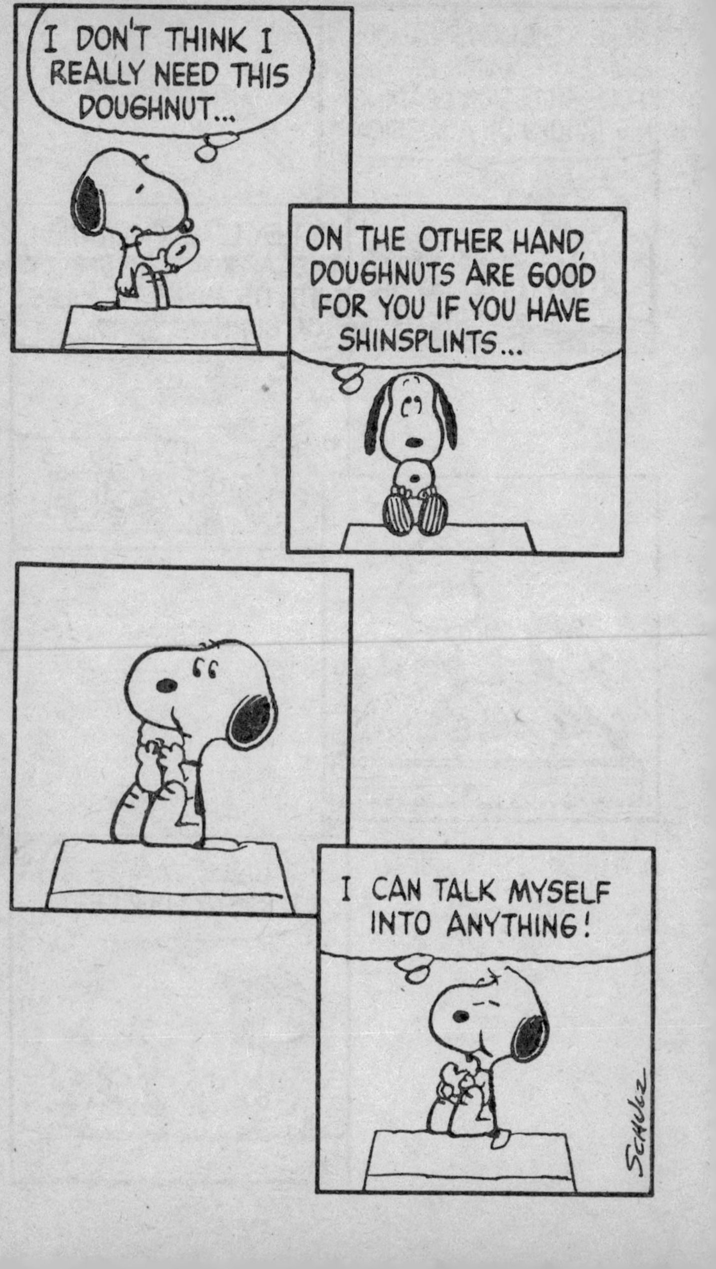
I DON'T THINK I REALLY NEED THIS DOUGHNUT...
ON THE OTHER HAND, DOUGHNUTS ARE GOOD FOR YOU IF YOU HAVE SHINSPLINTS...
I CAN TALK MYSELF INTO ANYTHING!
SCHULZ

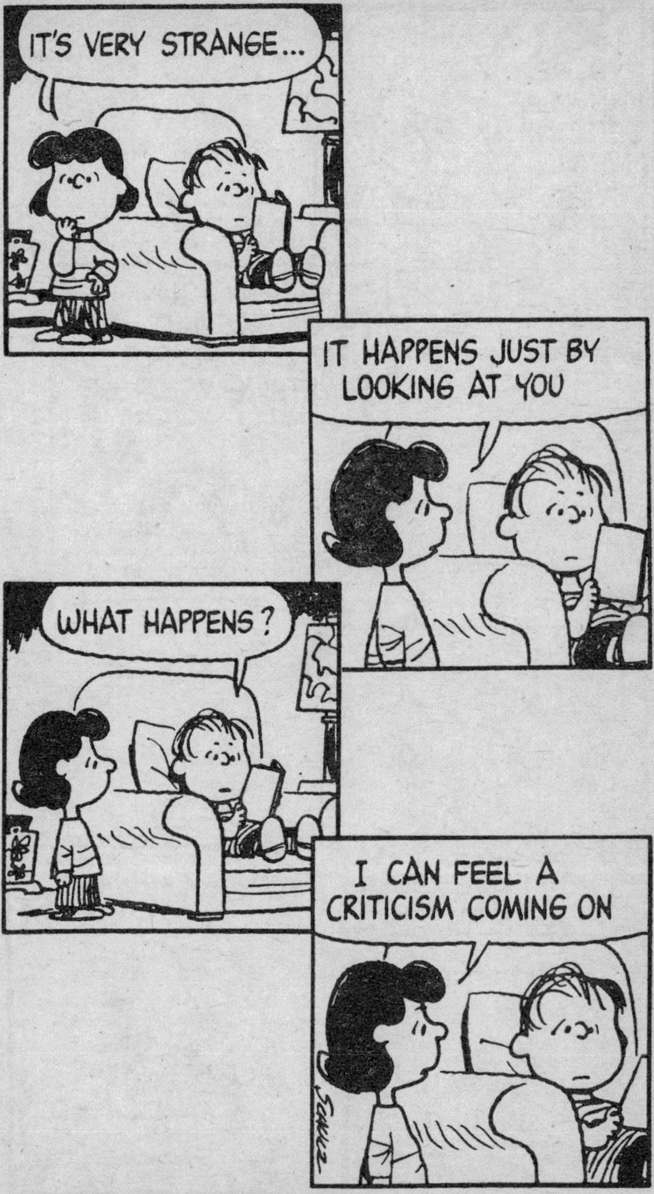
IT'S VERY STRANGE...
IT HAPPENS JUST BY LOOKING AT YOU
WHAT HAPPENS?
I CAN FEEL A CRITICISM COMING ON
SCHULZ

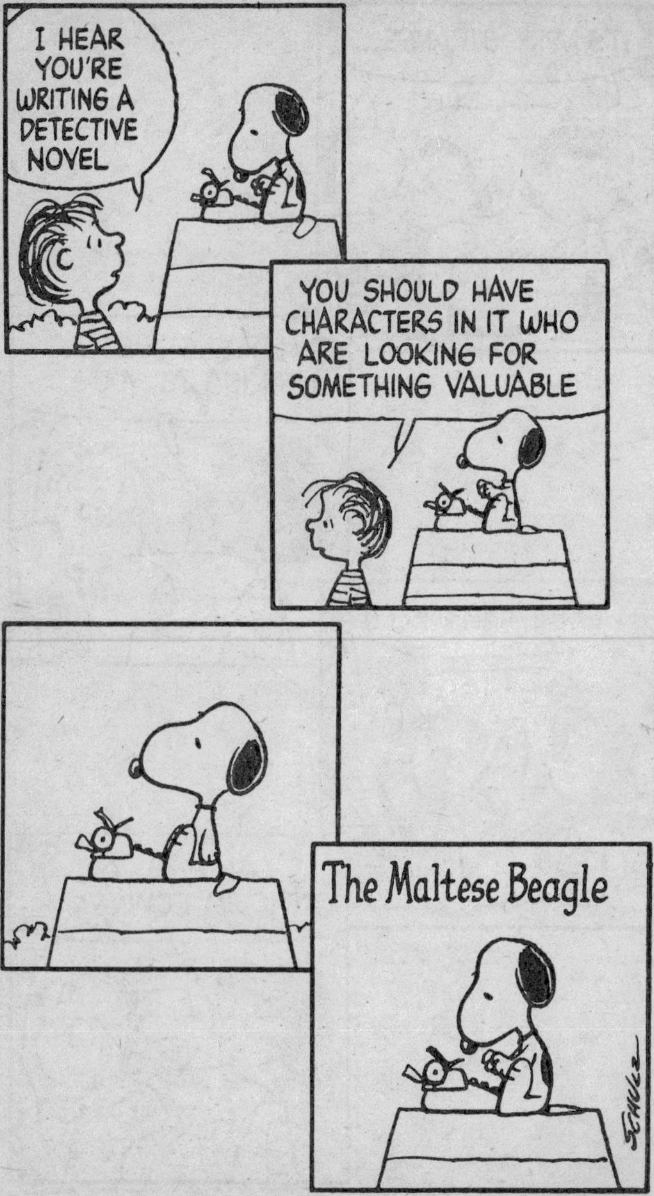
I HEAR YOU'RE WRITING A DETECTIVE NOVEL
YOU SHOULD HAVE CHARACTERS IN IT WHO ARE LOOKING FOR SOMETHING VALUABLE
The Maltese Beagle
SCHULZ

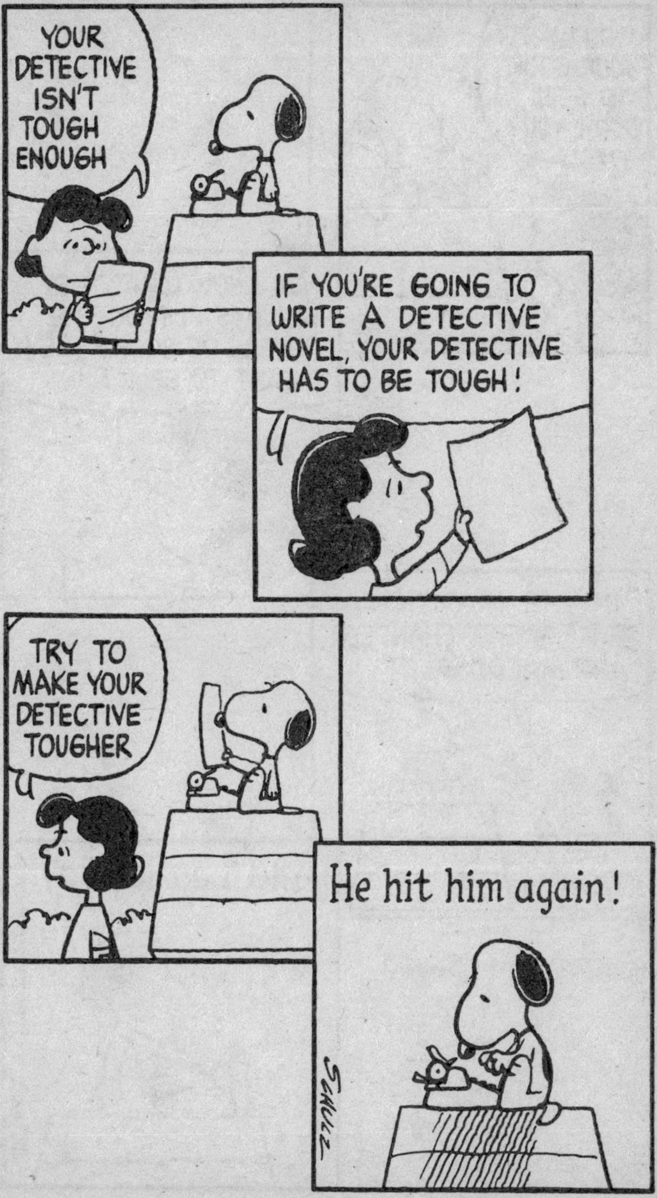
YOUR DETECTIVE ISN'T TOUGH ENOUGH
IF YOU'RE GOING TO WRITE A DETECTIVE NOVEL, YOUR DETECTIVE HAS TO BE TOUGH!
TRY TO MAKE YOUR DETECTIVE TOUGHER
He hit him again!
SCHULZ

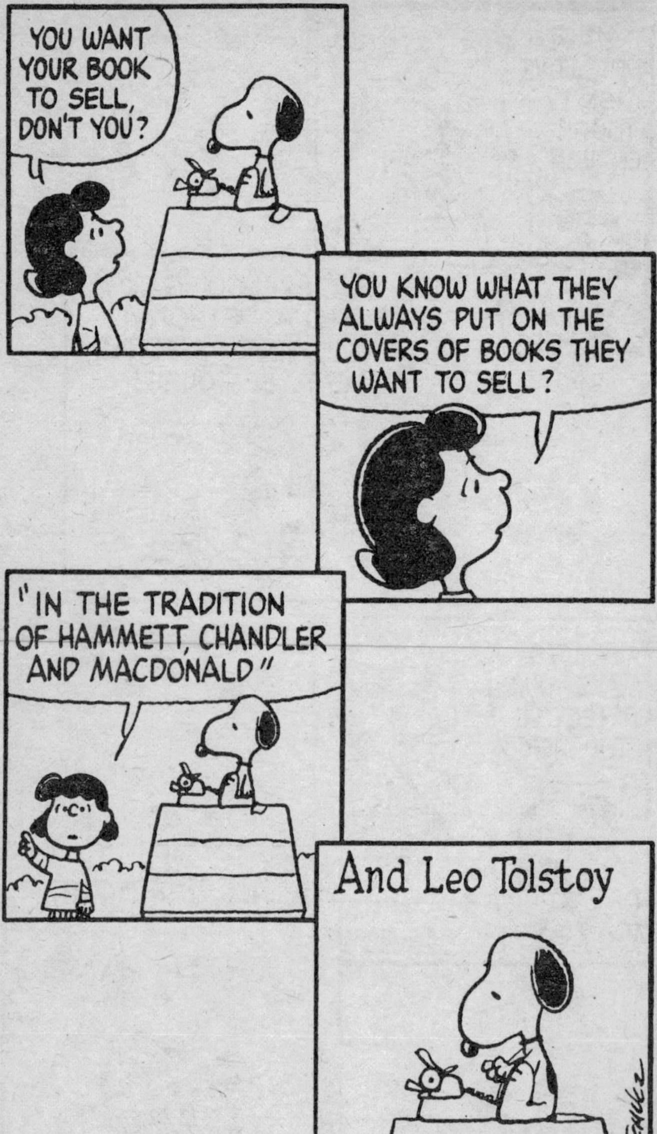
YOU WANT YOUR BOOK TO SELL, DON'T YOU?
YOU KNOW WHAT THEY ALWAYS PUT ON THE COVERS OF BOOKS THEY WANT TO SELL?
"IN THE TRADITION OF HAMMETT, CHANDLER AND MACDONALD"
And Leo Tolstoy
SCHULZ

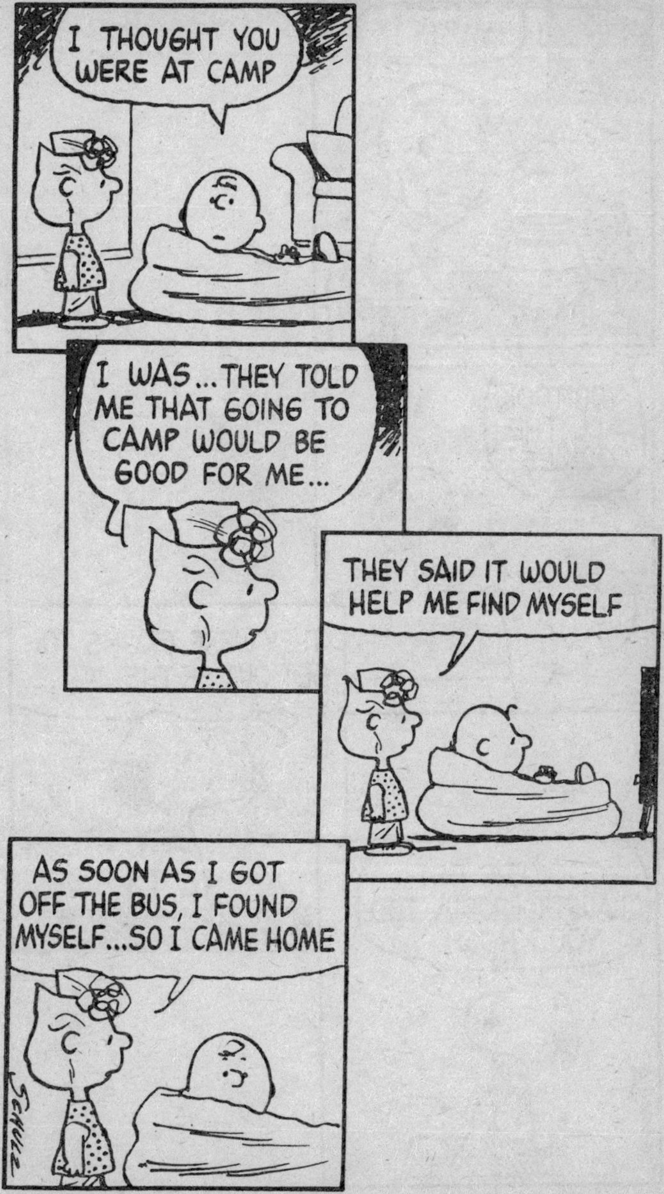
I THOUGHT YOU WERE AT CAMP
I WAS...THEY TOLD ME THAT GOING TO CAMP WOULD BE GOOD FOR ME...
THEY SAID IT WOULD HELP ME FIND MYSELF
AS SOON AS I GOT OFF THE BUS, I FOUND MYSELF...SO I CAME HOME
SCHULZ

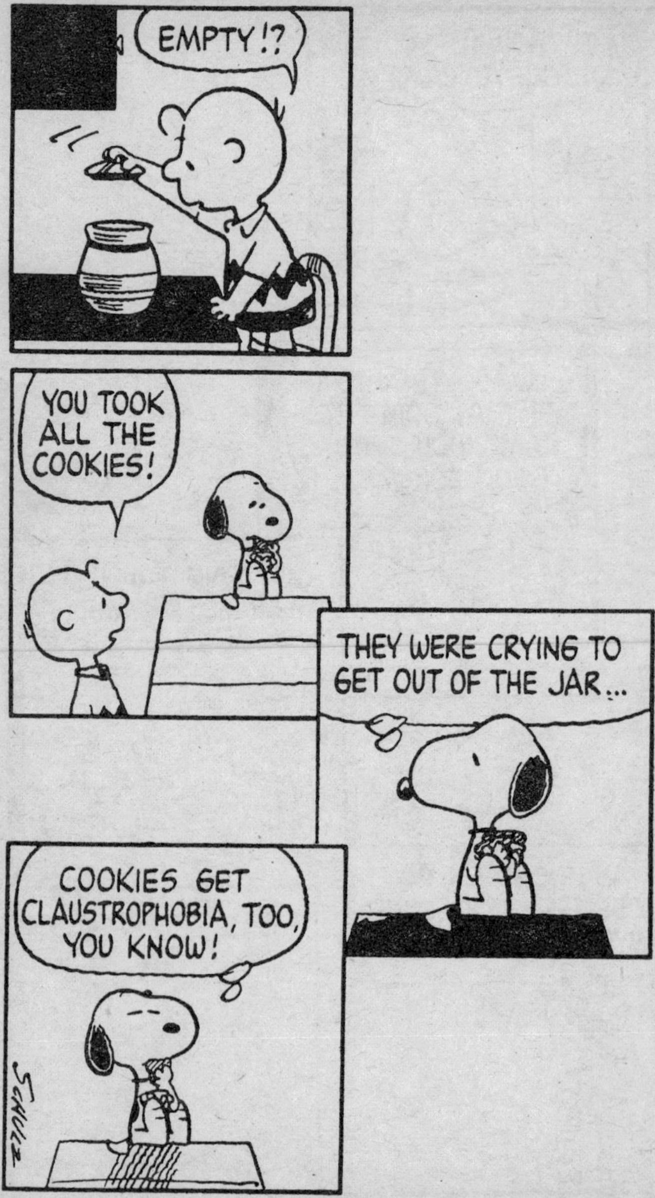
EMPTY!?
YOU TOOK ALL THE COOKIES!
THEY WERE CRYING TO GET OUT OF THE JAR...
COOKIES GET CLAUSTROPHOBIA, TOO, YOU KNOW!
SCHULZ

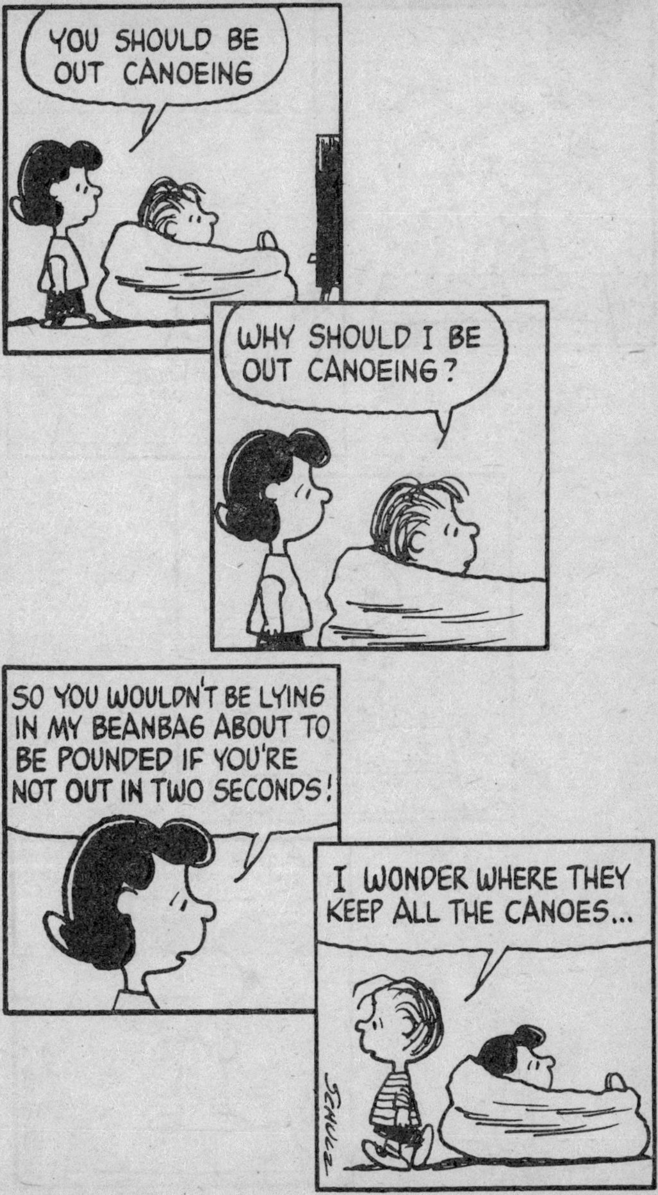
YOU SHOULD BE OUT CANOEING
WHY SHOULD I BE OUT CANOEING?
SO YOU WOULDN'T BE LYING IN MY BEANBAG ABOUT TO BE POUNDED IF YOU'RE NOT OUT IN TWO SECONDS!
I WONDER WHERE THEY KEEP ALL THE CANOES...
SCHULZ

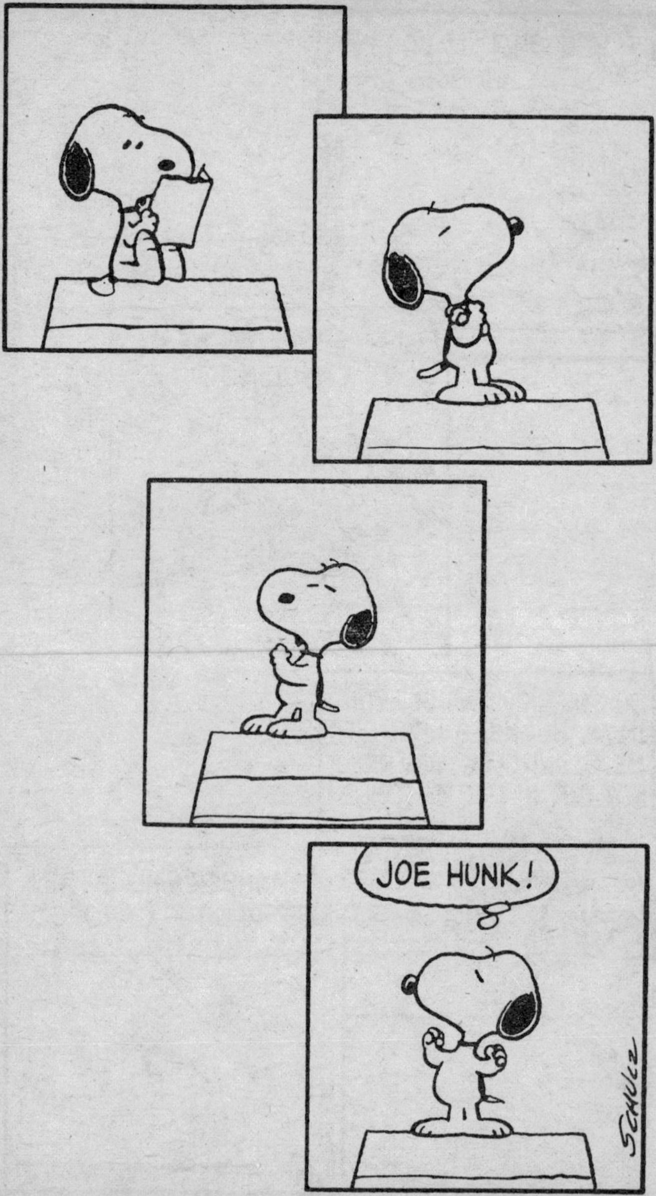
JOE HUNK!
SCHULZ

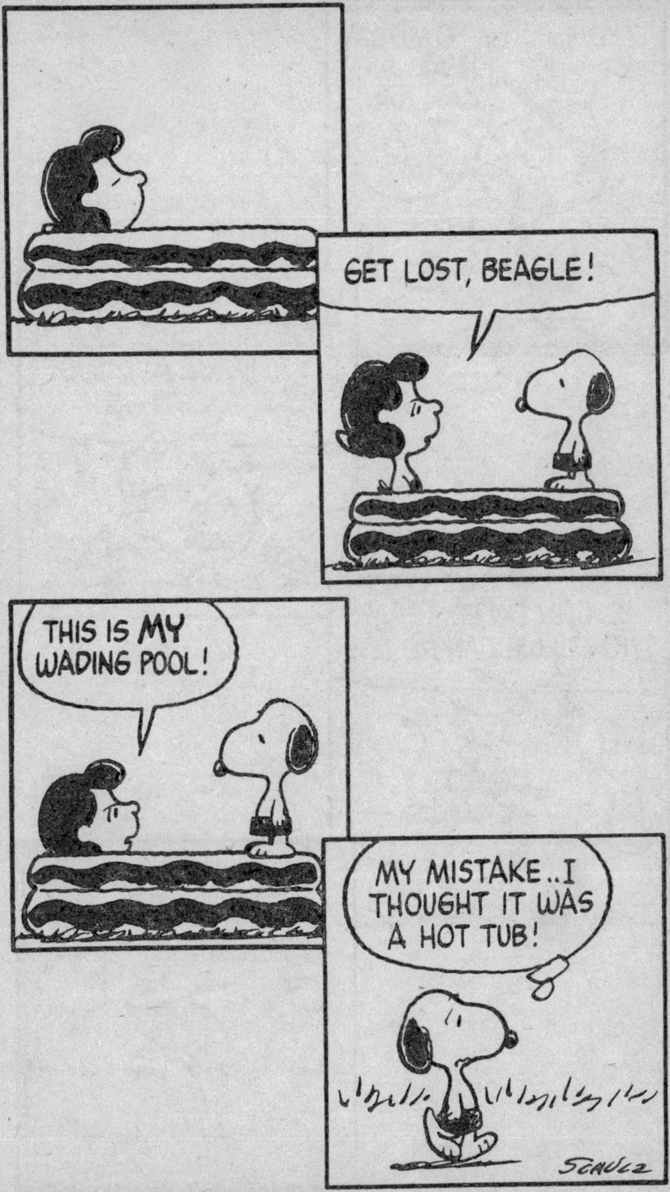
GET LOST, BEAGLE!
THIS IS MY WADING POOL!
MY MISTAKE..I THOUGHT IT WAS A HOT TUB!
SCHULZ

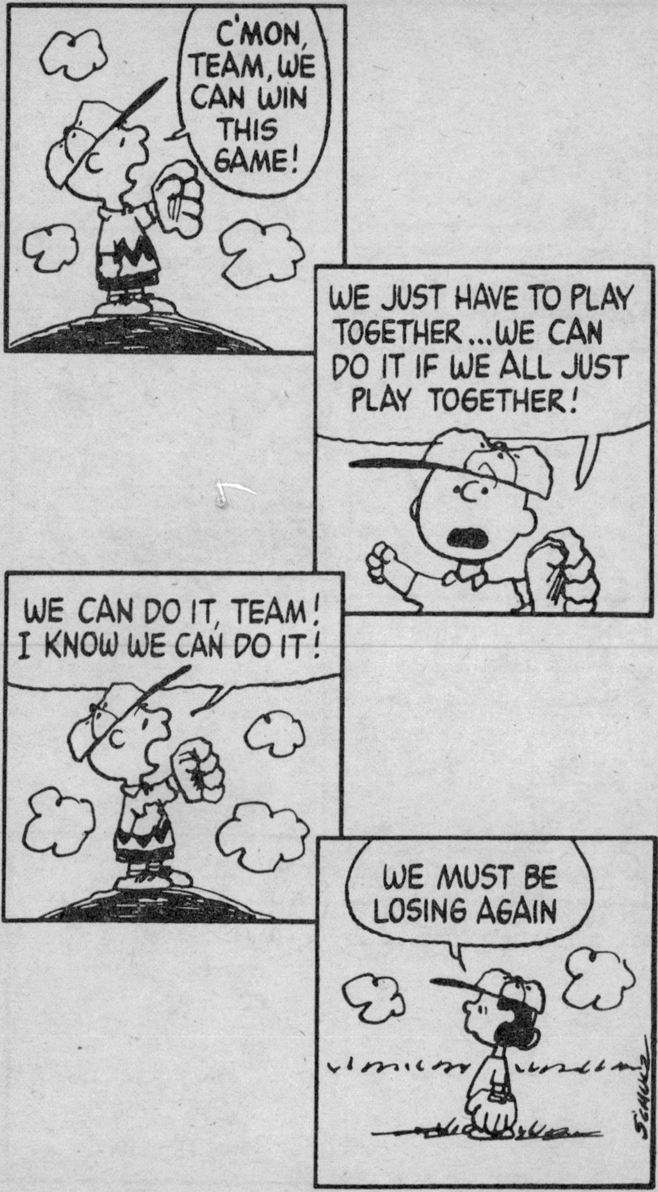
C'MON, TEAM, WE CAN WIN THIS GAME!
WE JUST HAVE TO PLAY TOGETHER...WE CAN DO IT IF WE ALL JUST PLAY TOGETHER!
WE CAN DO IT, TEAM! I KNOW WE CAN DO IT!
WE MUST BE LOSING AGAIN

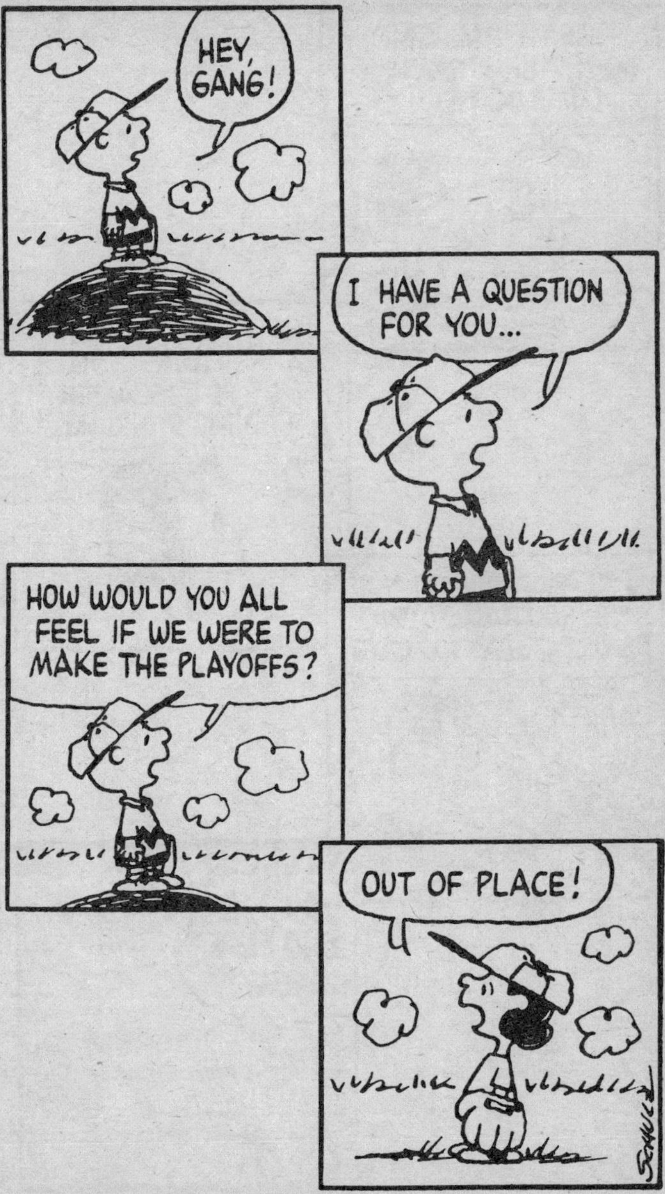
HEY, GANG!
I HAVE A QUESTION FOR YOU...
HOW WOULD YOU ALL FEEL IF WE WERE TO MAKE THE PLAYOFFS?
OUT OF PLACE!

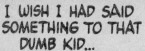

I WISH I HAD SAID SOMETHING TO THAT DUMB KID...

THE FRENCH HAVE A GOOD PHRASE, SIR... "ESPRIT DE L'ESCALIER"— "WIT OF THE STAIRWAY"

IT REFERS TO WHAT YOU WISH YOU HAD SAID BEFORE IT WAS TOO LATE

OH, YEAH? YOU AND WHO ELSE, DUMMY!?

ESPRIT DE L'ESCALIER, SIR...

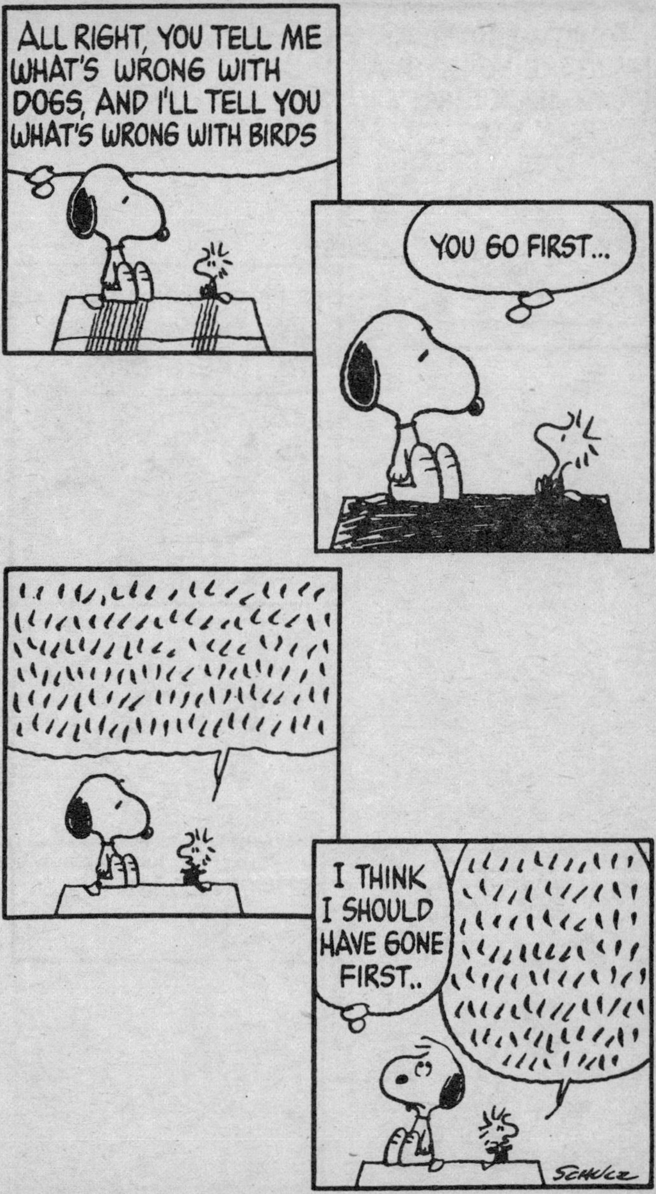
ALL RIGHT, YOU TELL ME WHAT'S WRONG WITH DOGS, AND I'LL TELL YOU WHAT'S WRONG WITH BIRDS
YOU GO FIRST...
I THINK I SHOULD HAVE GONE FIRST..
SCHULZ

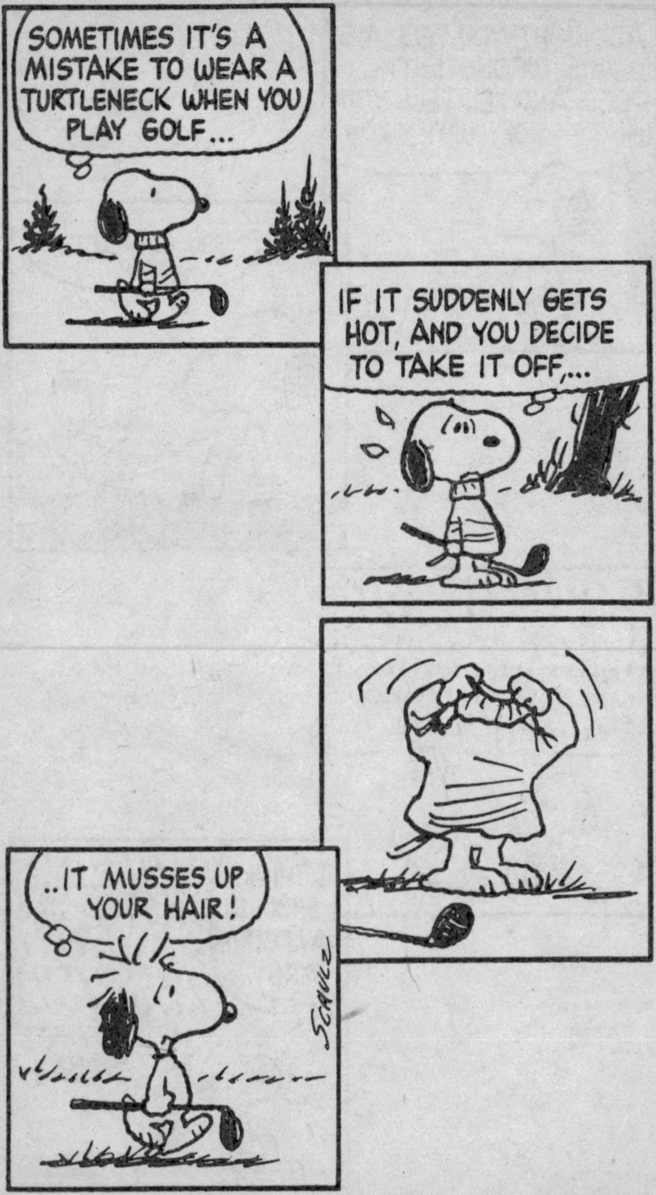
SOMETIMES IT'S A MISTAKE TO WEAR A TURTLENECK WHEN YOU PLAY GOLF...
IF IT SUDDENLY GETS HOT, AND YOU DECIDE TO TAKE IT OFF,...
..IT MUSSES UP YOUR HAIR!
SCHULZ

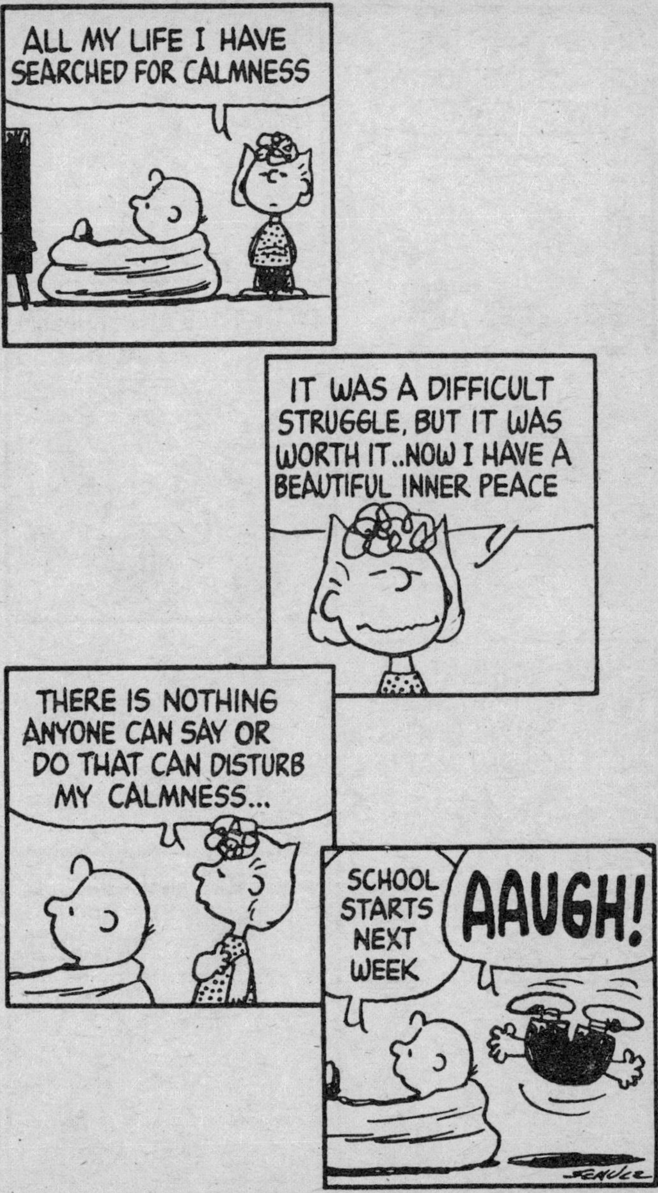
ALL MY LIFE I HAVE SEARCHED FOR CALMNESS
IT WAS A DIFFICULT STRUGGLE, BUT IT WAS WORTH IT..NOW I HAVE A BEAUTIFUL INNER PEACE
THERE IS NOTHING ANYONE CAN SAY OR DO THAT CAN DISTURB MY CALMNESS...
SCHOOL STARTS NEXT WEEK
AAUGH!

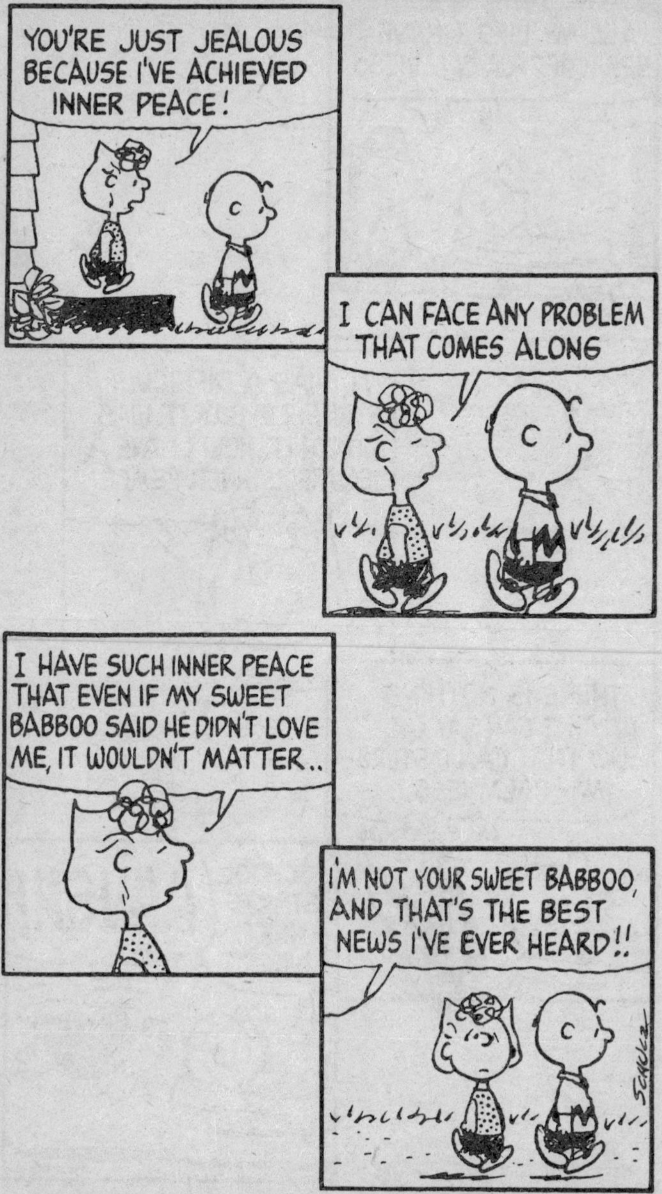
YOU'RE JUST JEALOUS BECAUSE I'VE ACHIEVED INNER PEACE!
I CAN FACE ANY PROBLEM THAT COMES ALONG
I HAVE SUCH INNER PEACE THAT EVEN IF MY SWEET BABBOO SAID HE DIDN'T LOVE ME, IT WOULDN'T MATTER..
I'M NOT YOUR SWEET BABBOO, AND THAT'S THE BEST NEWS I'VE EVER HEARD!!

I HATE EVERYTHING! I HATE THE WHOLE WORLD!
I THOUGHT YOU HAD INNER PEACE
I DO
BUT I STILL HAVE OUTER OBNOXIOUSNESS!

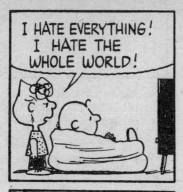

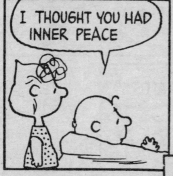

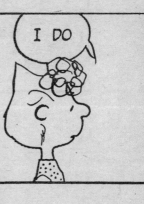

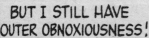

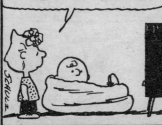

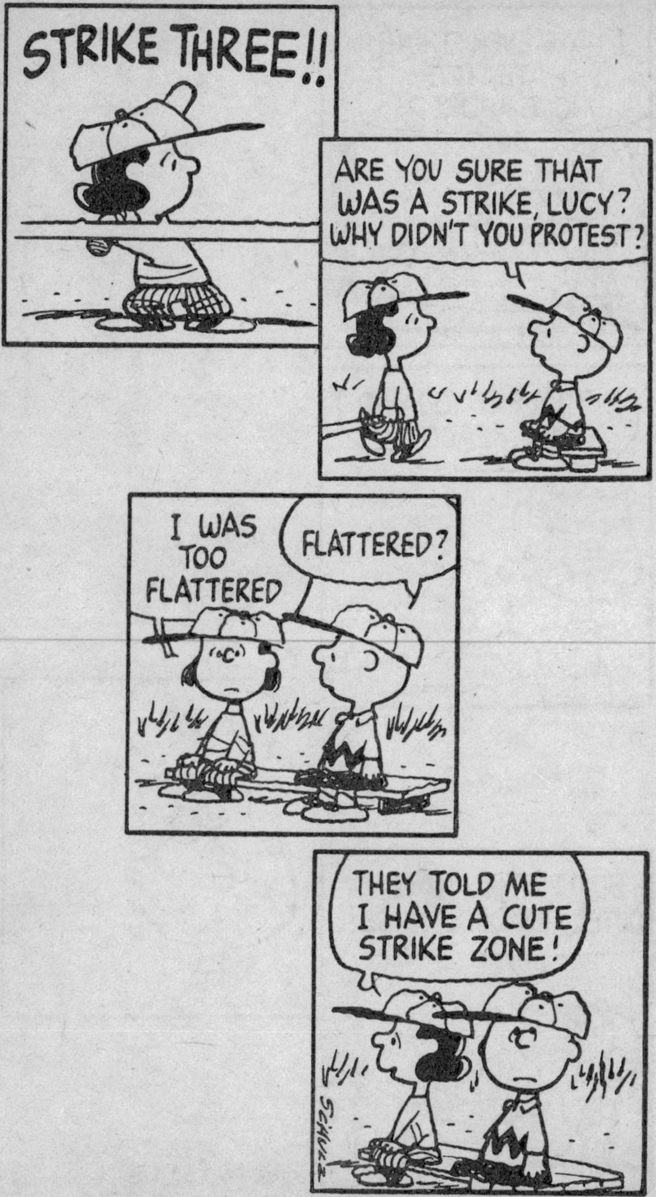
STRIKE THREE!!
ARE YOU SURE THAT WAS A STRIKE, LUCY? WHY DIDN'T YOU PROTEST?
I WAS TOO FLATTERED
FLATTERED?
THEY TOLD ME I HAVE A CUTE STRIKE ZONE!
SCHULZ

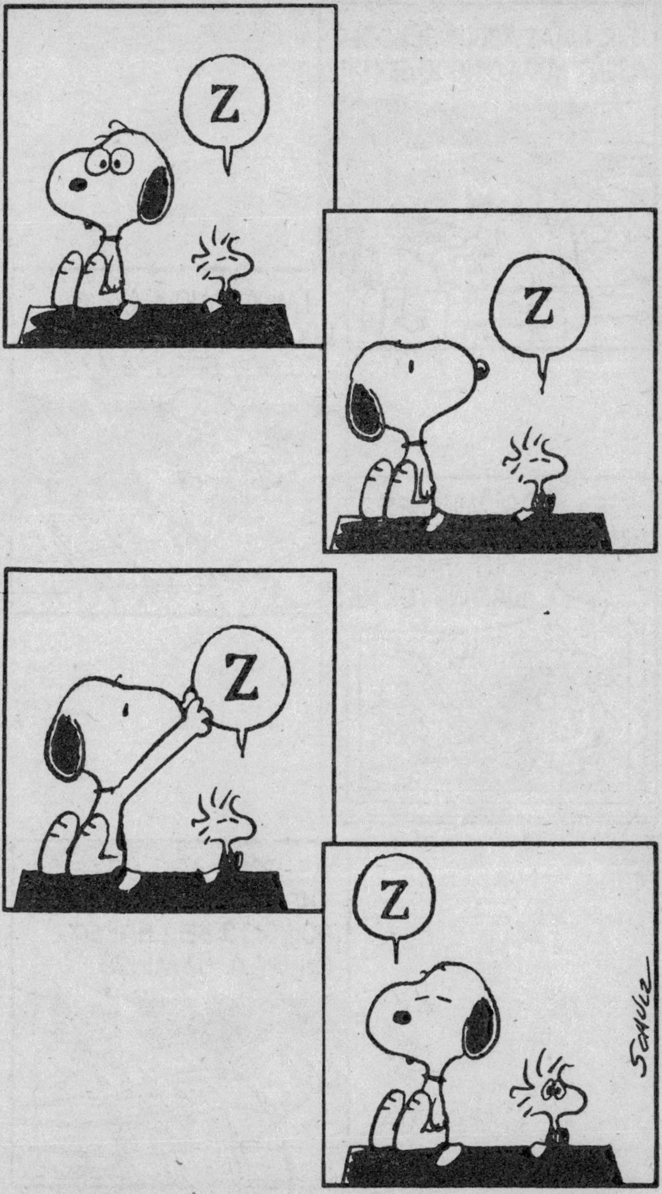
Z
Z
Z
Z

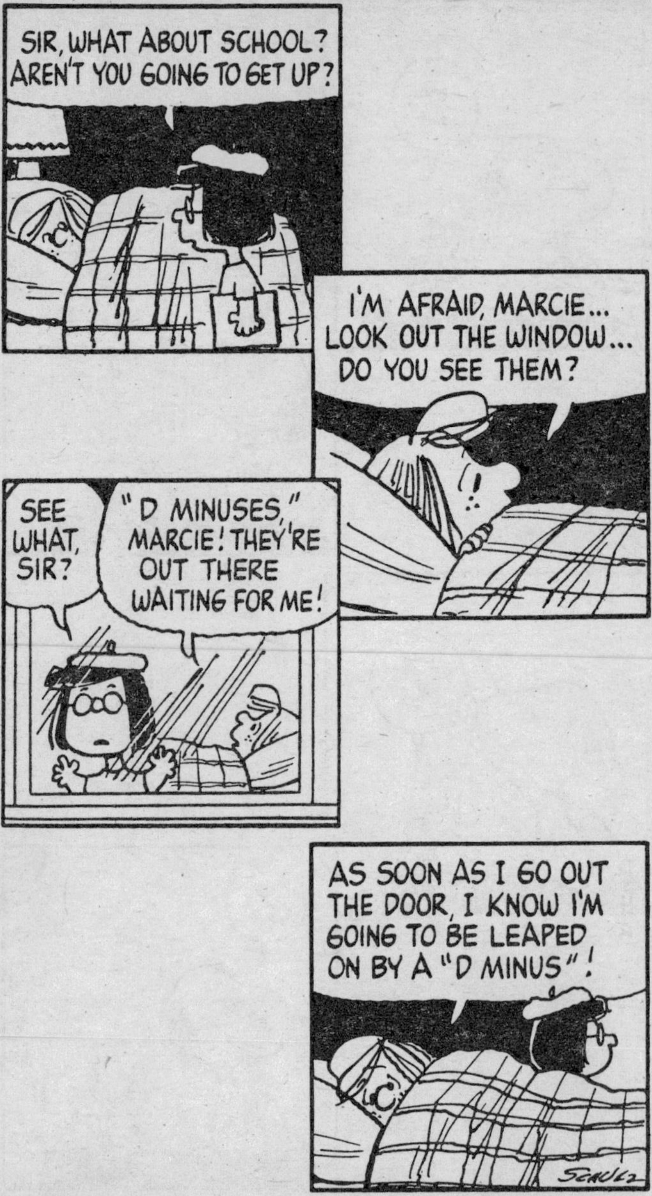
SIR, WHAT ABOUT SCHOOL? AREN'T YOU GOING TO GET UP?
I'M AFRAID, MARCIE... LOOK OUT THE WINDOW... DO YOU SEE THEM?
SEE WHAT, SIR?
"D MINUSES," MARCIE! THEY'RE OUT THERE WAITING FOR ME!
AS SOON AS I GO OUT THE DOOR, I KNOW I'M GOING TO BE LEAPED ON BY A "D MINUS"!
SCHULZ

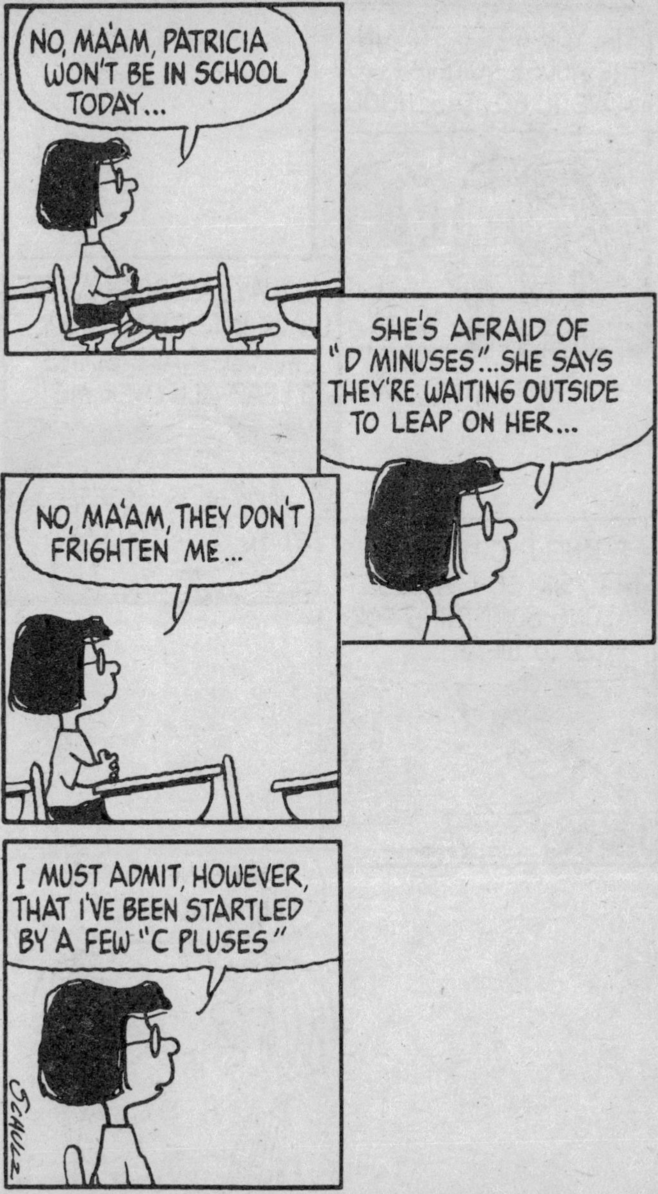
NO, MA'AM, PATRICIA WON'T BE IN SCHOOL TODAY...
SHE'S AFRAID OF "D MINUSES"...SHE SAYS THEY'RE WAITING OUTSIDE TO LEAP ON HER...
NO, MA'AM, THEY DON'T FRIGHTEN ME...
I MUST ADMIT, HOWEVER, THAT I'VE BEEN STARTLED BY A FEW "C PLUSES"
SCHULZ

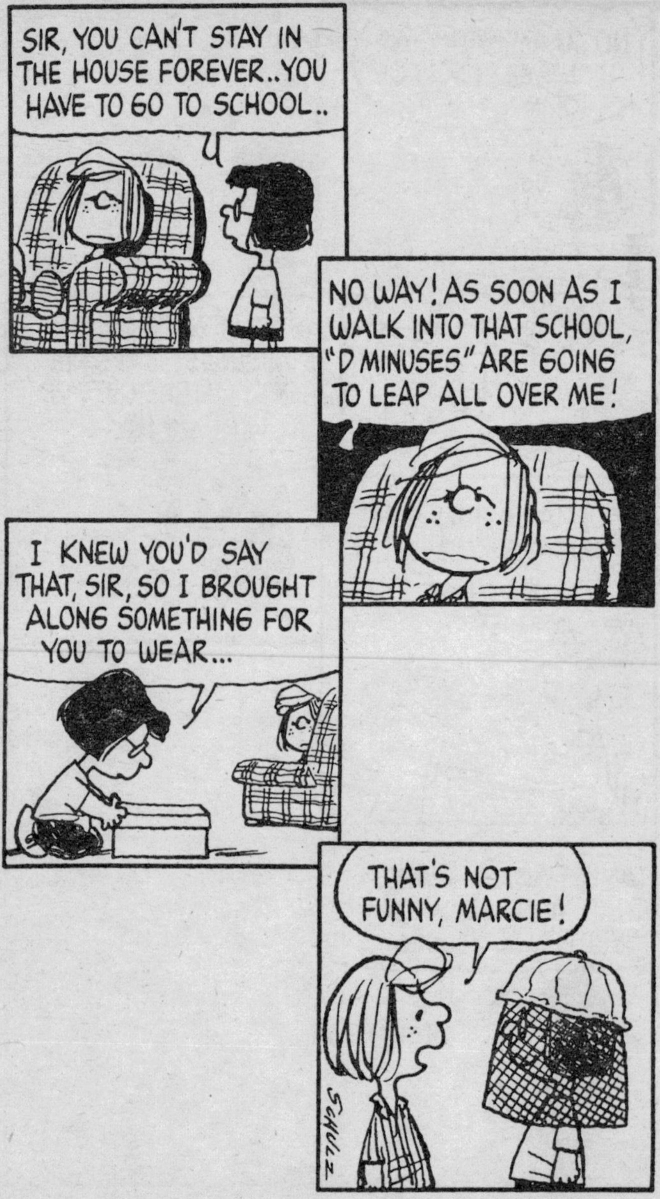
SIR, YOU CAN'T STAY IN THE HOUSE FOREVER..YOU HAVE TO GO TO SCHOOL..
NO WAY! AS SOON AS I WALK INTO THAT SCHOOL, "D MINUSES" ARE GOING TO LEAP ALL OVER ME!
I KNEW YOU'D SAY THAT, SIR, SO I BROUGHT ALONG SOMETHING FOR YOU TO WEAR...
THAT'S NOT FUNNY, MARCIE!
SCHULZ

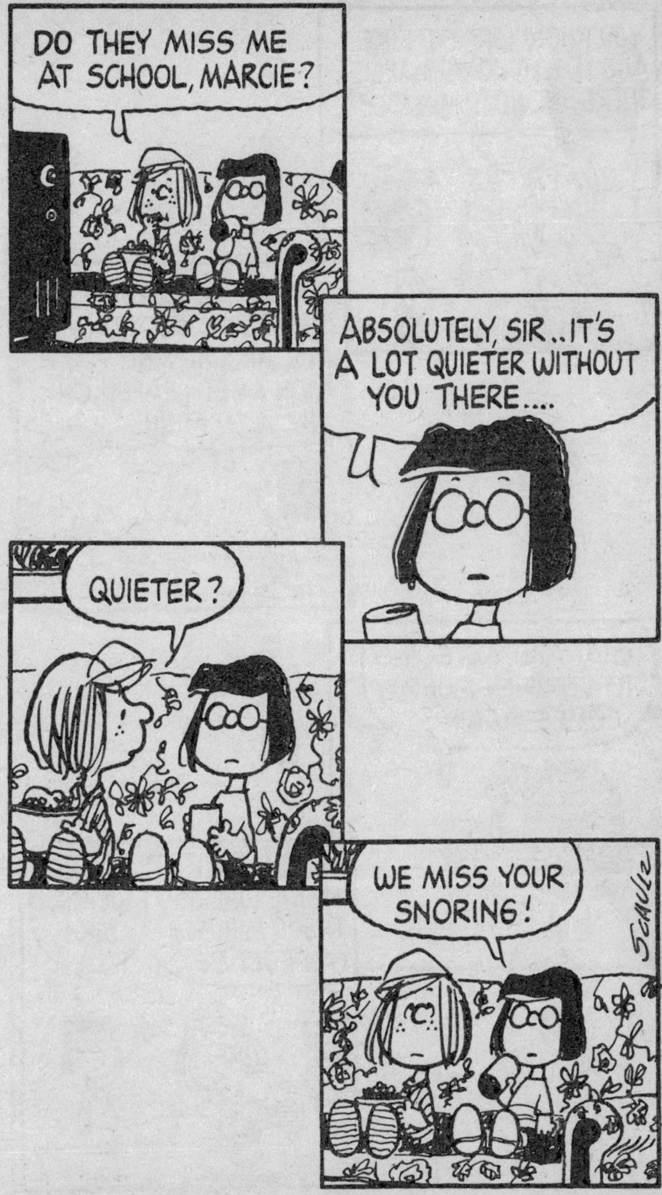
DO THEY MISS ME AT SCHOOL, MARCIE?
ABSOLUTELY, SIR..IT'S A LOT QUIETER WITHOUT YOU THERE....
QUIETER?
WE MISS YOUR SNORING!
SCHULZ

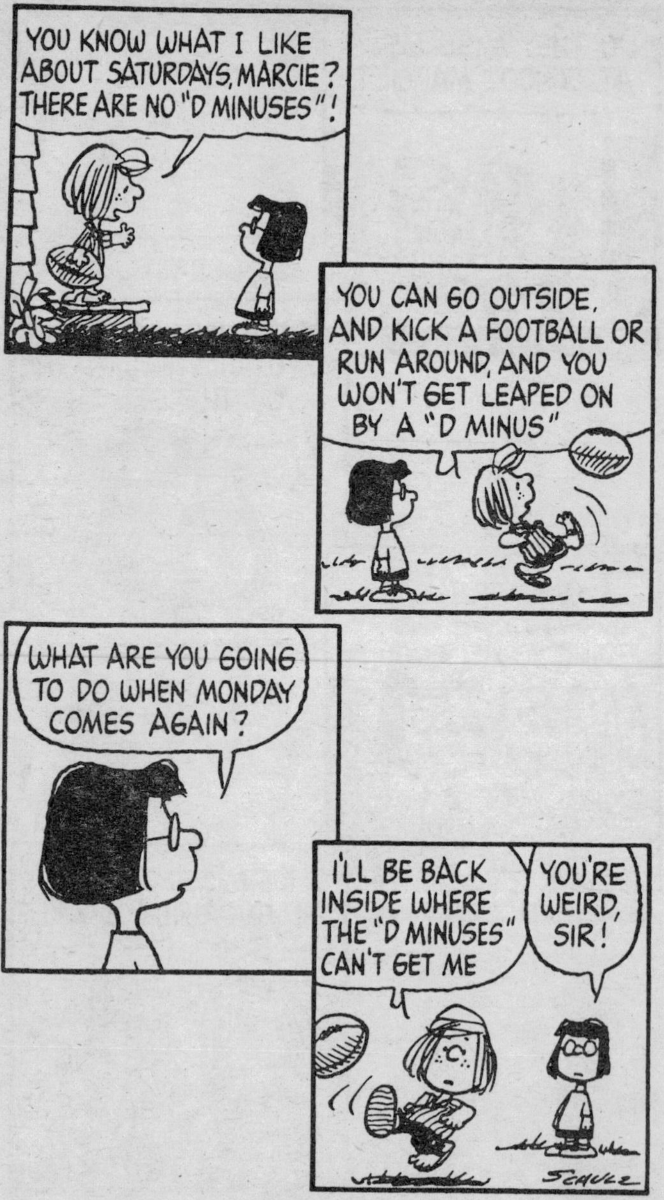
YOU KNOW WHAT I LIKE ABOUT SATURDAYS, MARCIE? THERE ARE NO "D MINUSES"!
YOU CAN GO OUTSIDE, AND KICK A FOOTBALL OR RUN AROUND, AND YOU WON'T GET LEAPED ON BY A "D MINUS"
WHAT ARE YOU GOING TO DO WHEN MONDAY COMES AGAIN?
I'LL BE BACK INSIDE WHERE THE "D MINUSES" CAN'T GET ME
YOU'RE WEIRD, SIR!
SCHULZ

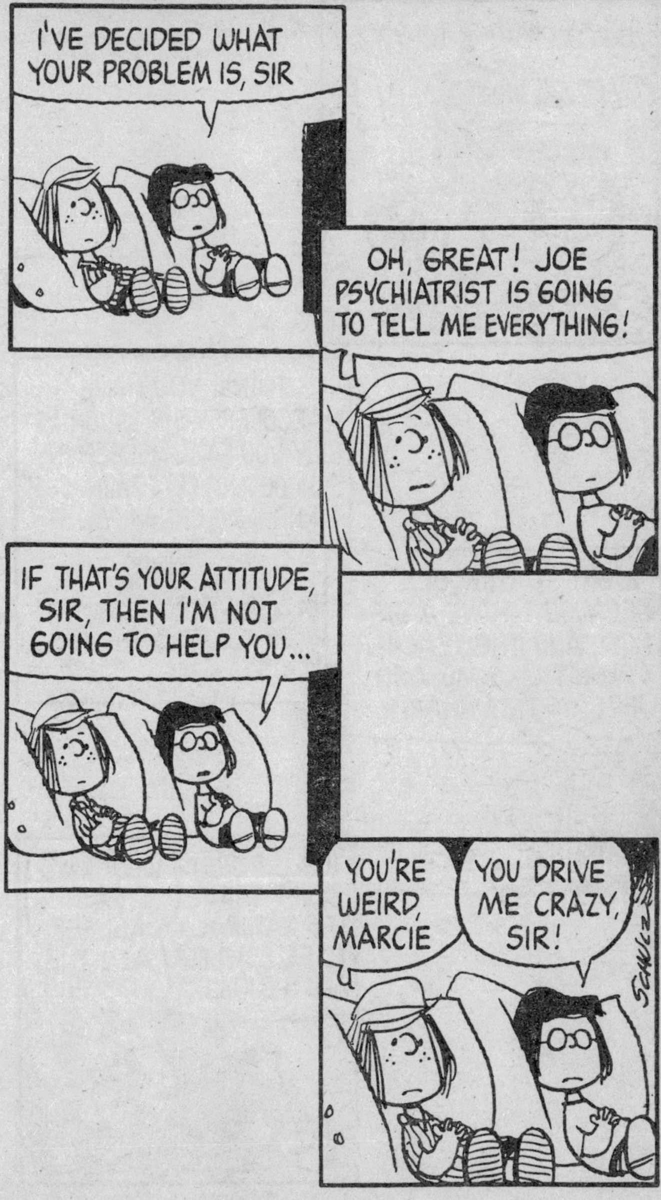
I'VE DECIDED WHAT YOUR PROBLEM IS, SIR
OH, GREAT! JOE PSYCHIATRIST IS GOING TO TELL ME EVERYTHING!
IF THAT'S YOUR ATTITUDE, SIR, THEN I'M NOT GOING TO HELP YOU...
YOU'RE WEIRD, MARCIE
YOU DRIVE ME CRAZY, SIR!
SCHULZ

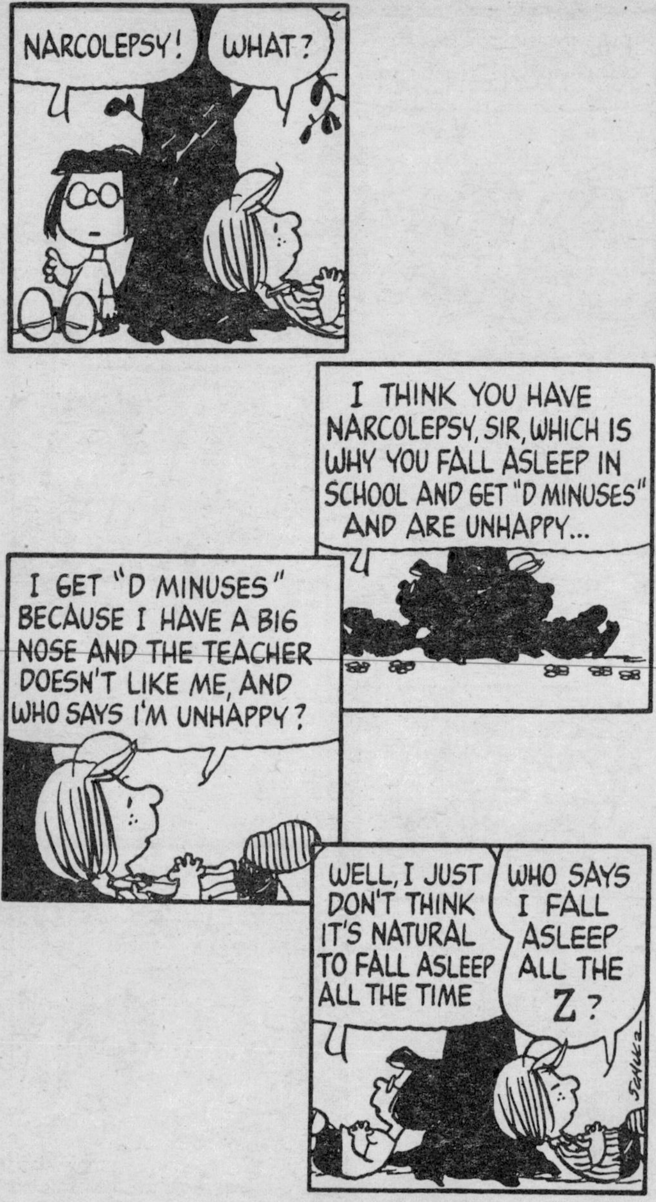
NARCOLEPSY!
WHAT?
I THINK YOU HAVE NARCOLEPSY, SIR, WHICH IS WHY YOU FALL ASLEEP IN SCHOOL AND GET "D MINUSES" AND ARE UNHAPPY...
I GET "D MINUSES" BECAUSE I HAVE A BIG NOSE AND THE TEACHER DOESN'T LIKE ME, AND WHO SAYS I'M UNHAPPY?
WELL, I JUST DON'T THINK IT'S NATURAL TO FALL ASLEEP ALL THE TIME
WHO SAYS I FALL ASLEEP ALL THE Z?
SCHULZ

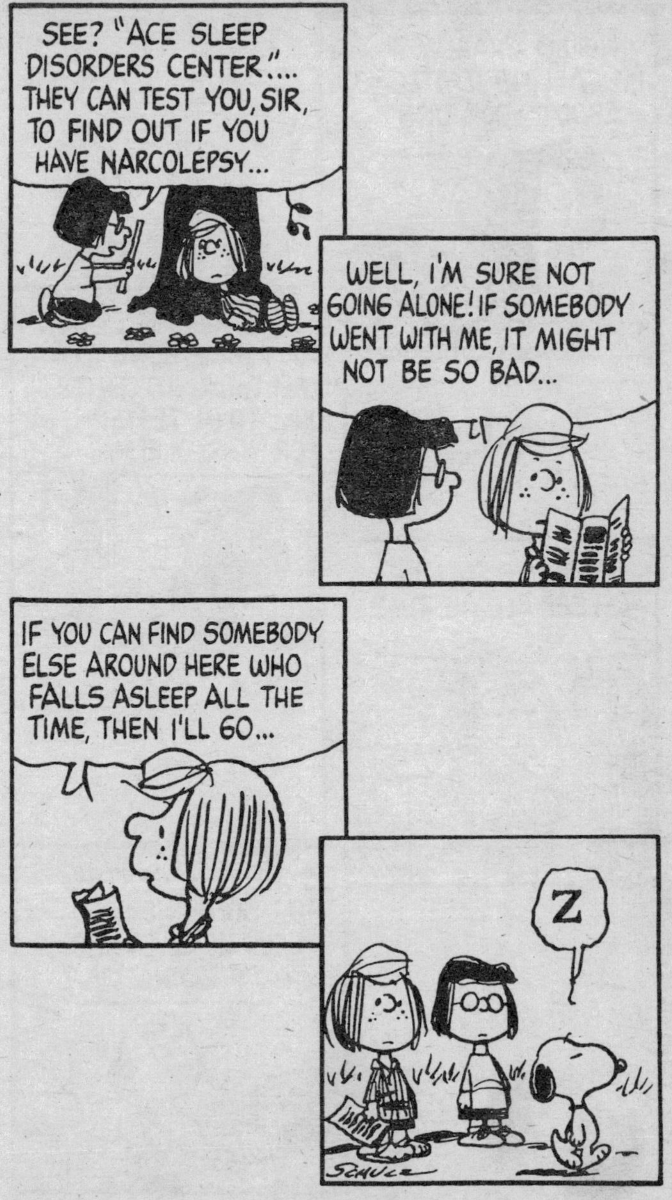

SEE? "ACE SLEEP DISORDERS CENTER."... THEY CAN TEST YOU, SIR, TO FIND OUT IF YOU HAVE NARCOLEPSY...
WELL, I'M SURE NOT GOING ALONE! IF SOMEBODY WENT WITH ME, IT MIGHT NOT BE SO BAD...
IF YOU CAN FIND SOMEBODY ELSE AROUND HERE WHO FALLS ASLEEP ALL THE TIME, THEN I'LL GO...
Z
SCHULZ

HELLO, CHARLES? I'M CALLING TO TELL YOU ABOUT YOUR DOG

SNOOPY AND PEPPERMINT PATTY HAVE GONE TO A "SLEEP DISORDERS CENTER"... WHY? TO BE TESTED FOR "NARCOLEPSY"

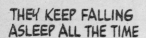

THEY KEEP FALLING ASLEEP ALL THE TIME

IS THERE A CENTER FOR SOMEONE WHO FEELS HE NEVER KNOWS WHAT'S GOING ON?

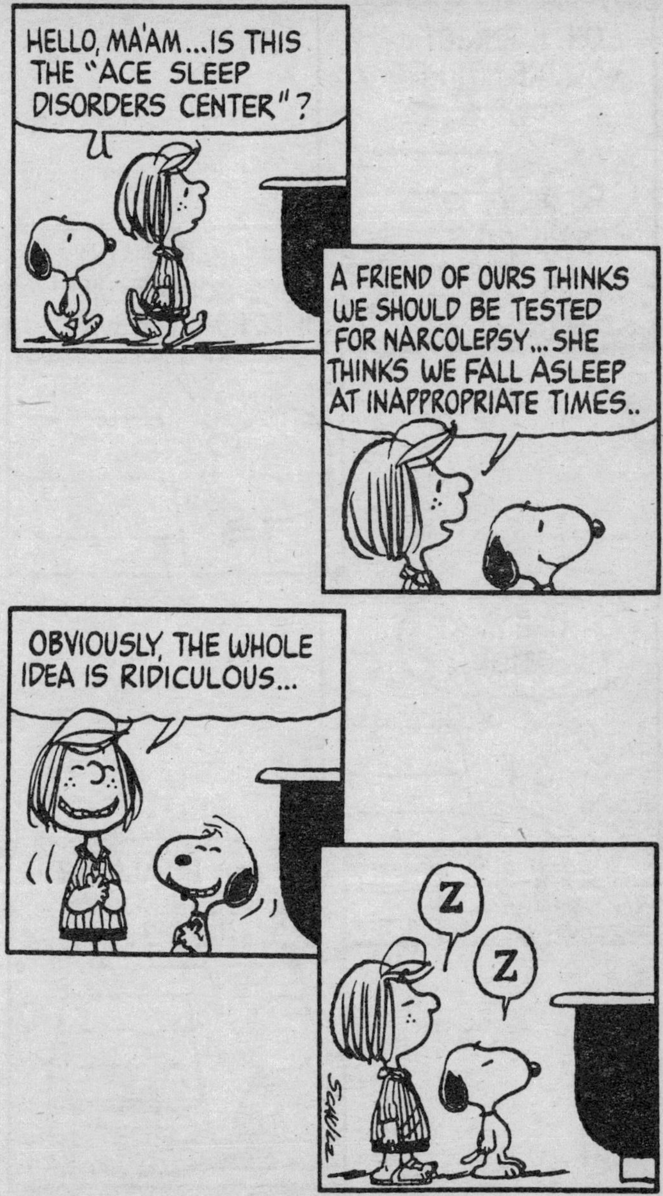
HELLO, MA'AM...IS THIS THE "ACE SLEEP DISORDERS CENTER"?
A FRIEND OF OURS THINKS WE SHOULD BE TESTED FOR NARCOLEPSY...SHE THINKS WE FALL ASLEEP AT INAPPROPRIATE TIMES..
OBVIOUSLY, THE WHOLE IDEA IS RIDICULOUS...
Z
Z
SCHULZ

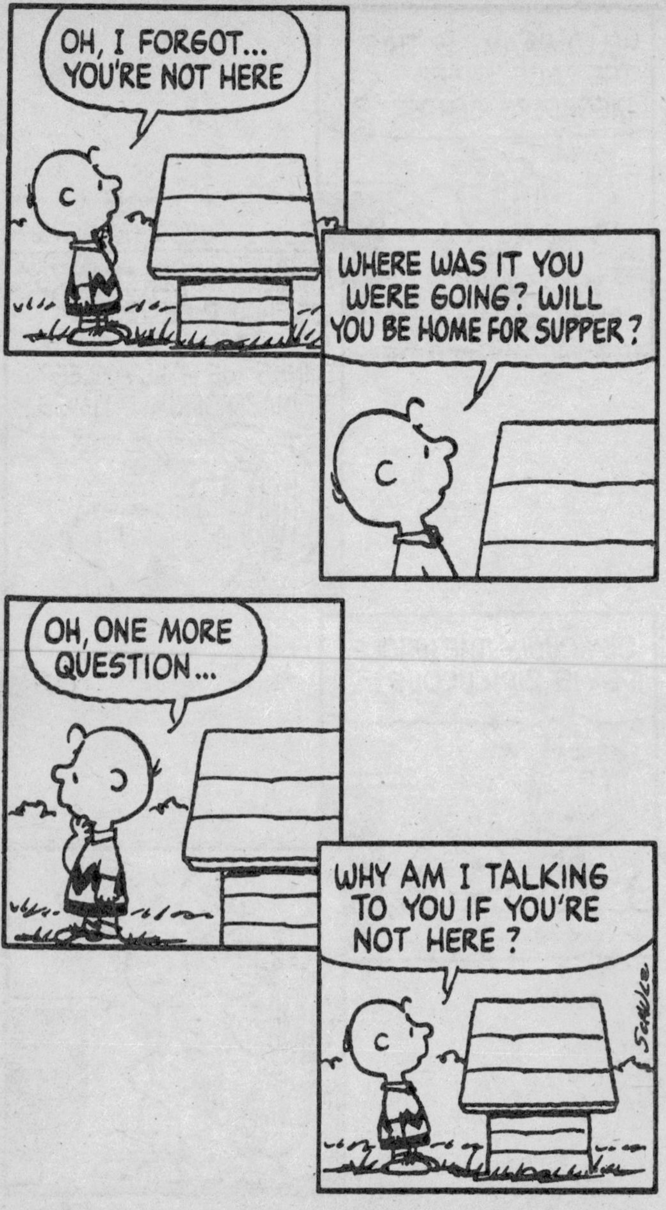
OH, I FORGOT... YOU'RE NOT HERE
WHERE WAS IT YOU WERE GOING? WILL YOU BE HOME FOR SUPPER?
OH, ONE MORE QUESTION...
WHY AM I TALKING TO YOU IF YOU'RE NOT HERE?
SCHULZ

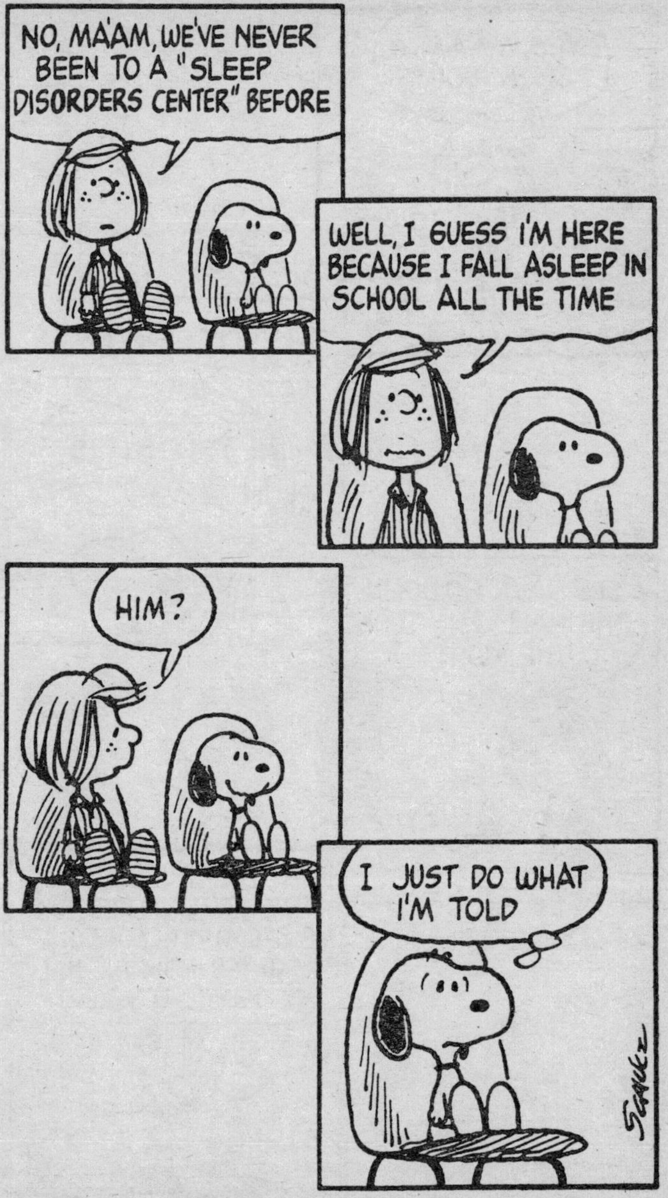
NO, MA'AM, WE'VE NEVER BEEN TO A "SLEEP DISORDERS CENTER" BEFORE
WELL, I GUESS I'M HERE BECAUSE I FALL ASLEEP IN SCHOOL ALL THE TIME
HIM?
I JUST DO WHAT I'M TOLD
SCHULZ

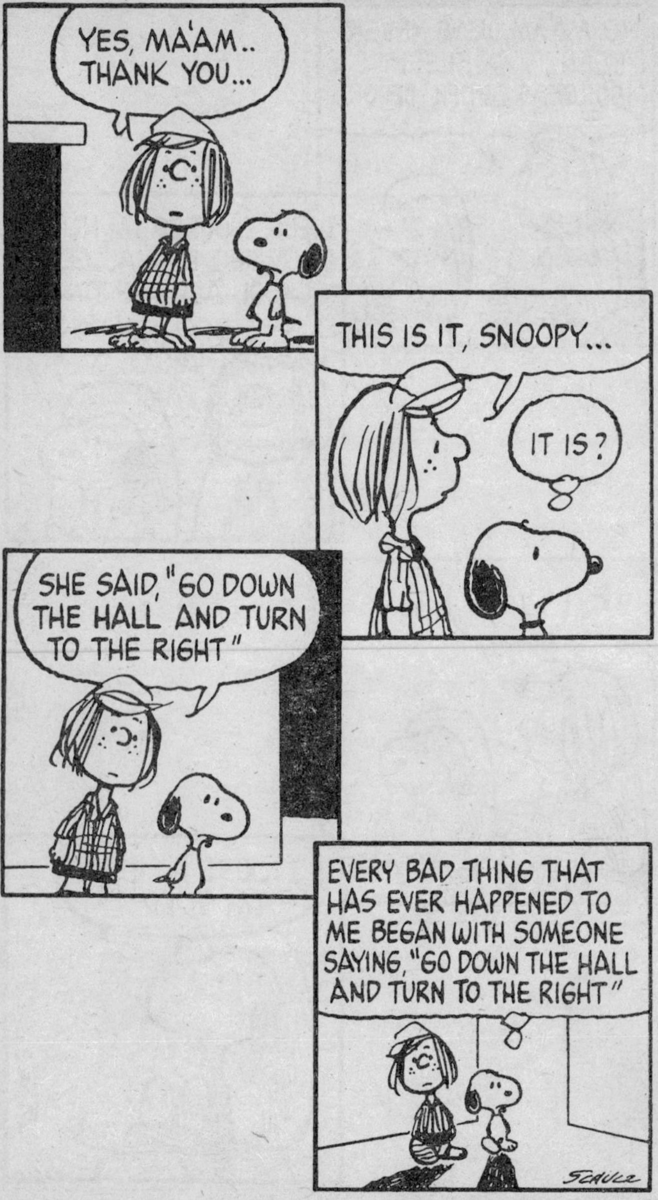
YES, MA'AM.. THANK YOU...
THIS IS IT, SNOOPY...
IT IS?
SHE SAID, "GO DOWN THE HALL AND TURN TO THE RIGHT"
EVERY BAD THING THAT HAS EVER HAPPENED TO ME BEGAN WITH SOMEONE SAYING, "GO DOWN THE HALL AND TURN TO THE RIGHT"
SCHULZ

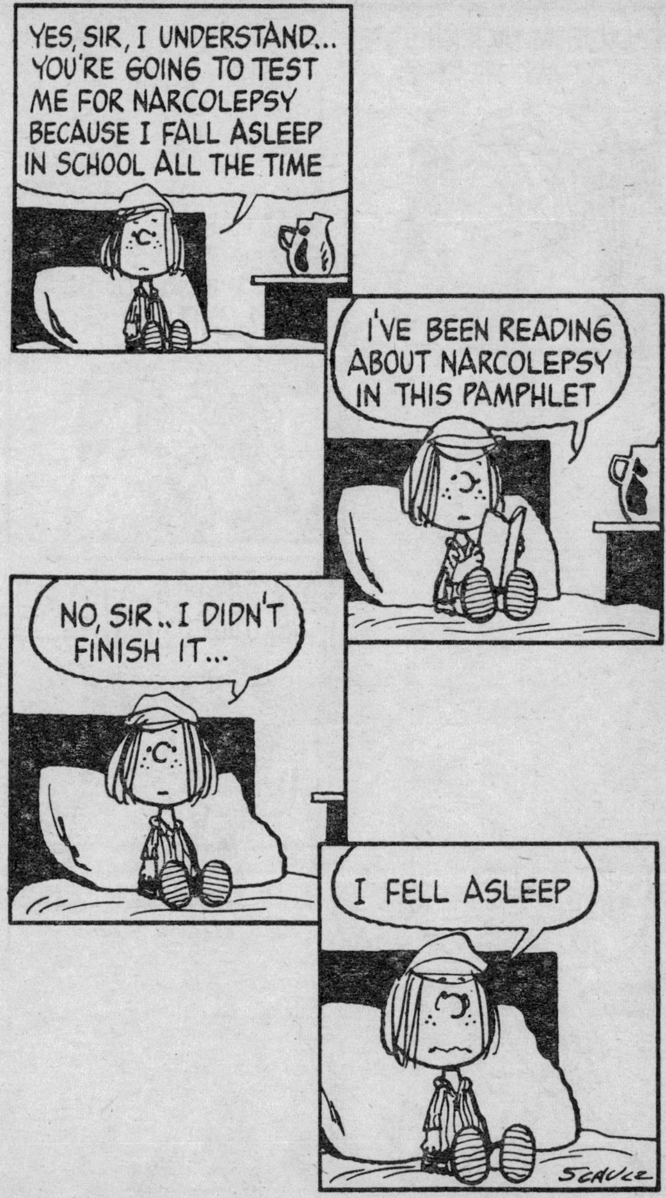
YES, SIR, I UNDERSTAND... YOU'RE GOING TO TEST ME FOR NARCOLEPSY BECAUSE I FALL ASLEEP IN SCHOOL ALL THE TIME
I'VE BEEN READING ABOUT NARCOLEPSY IN THIS PAMPHLET
NO, SIR.. I DIDN'T FINISH IT...
I FELL ASLEEP
SCHULZ

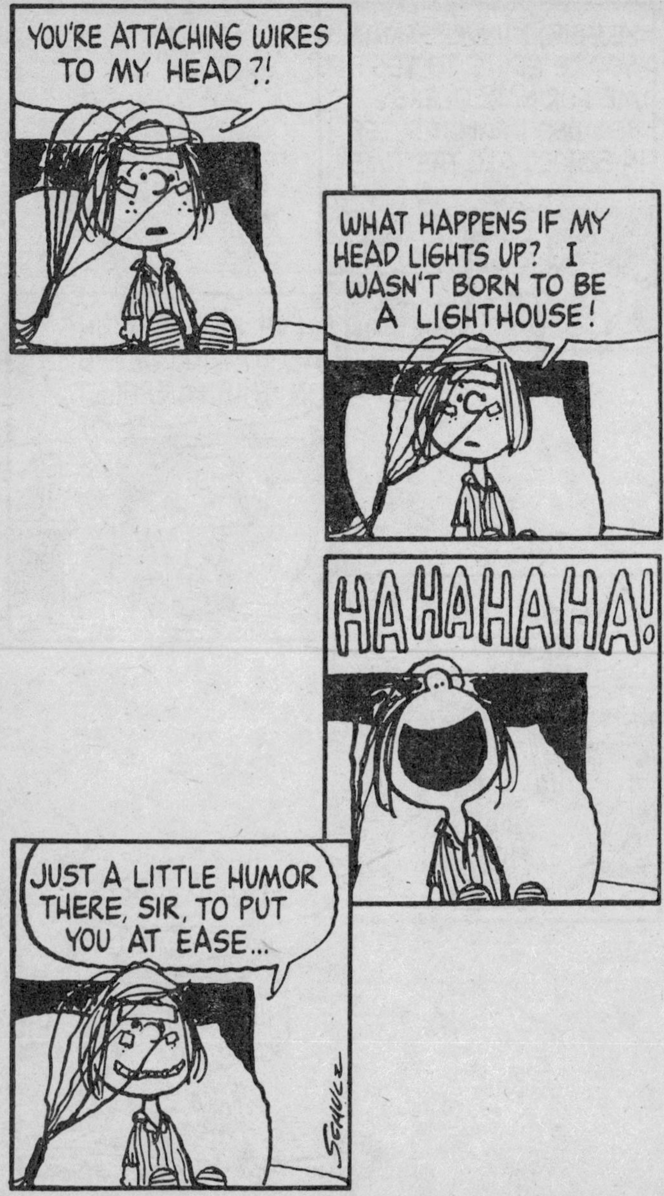
YOU'RE ATTACHING WIRES TO MY HEAD ?!
WHAT HAPPENS IF MY HEAD LIGHTS UP? I WASN'T BORN TO BE A LIGHTHOUSE!
HAHAHAHA!
JUST A LITTLE HUMOR THERE, SIR, TO PUT YOU AT EASE...
SCHULZ

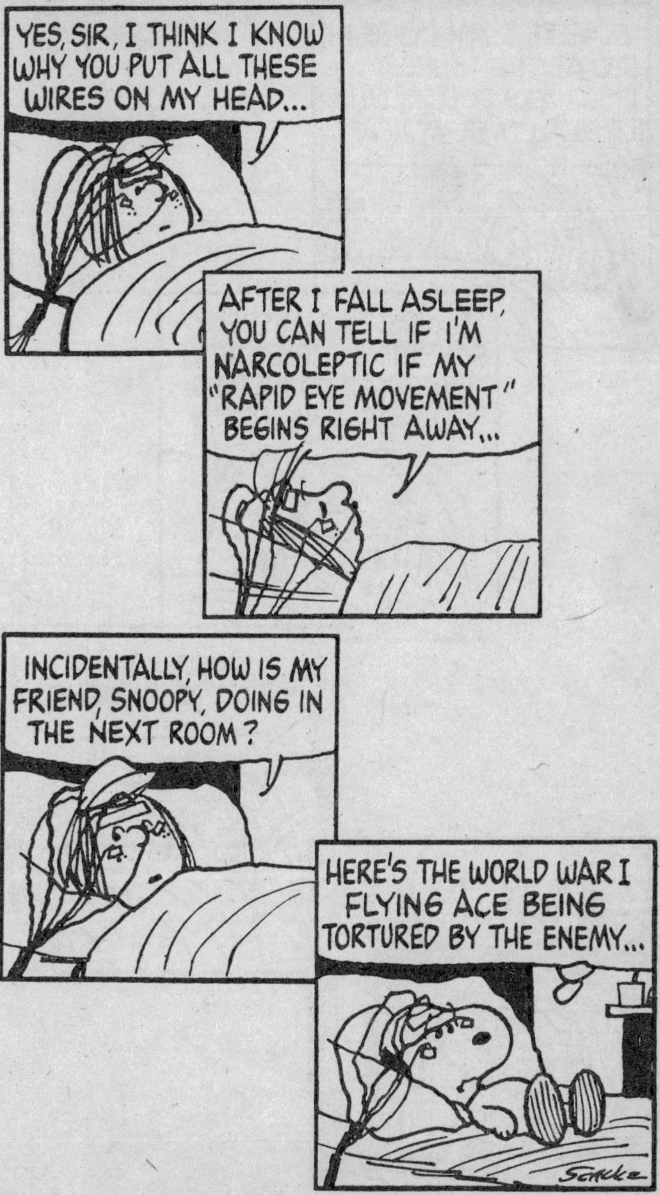
YES, SIR, I THINK I KNOW WHY YOU PUT ALL THESE WIRES ON MY HEAD...
AFTER I FALL ASLEEP, YOU CAN TELL IF I'M NARCOLEPTIC IF MY "RAPID EYE MOVEMENT" BEGINS RIGHT AWAY...
INCIDENTALLY, HOW IS MY FRIEND, SNOOPY, DOING IN THE NEXT ROOM?
HERE'S THE WORLD WAR I FLYING ACE BEING TORTURED BY THE ENEMY...
SCHULZ

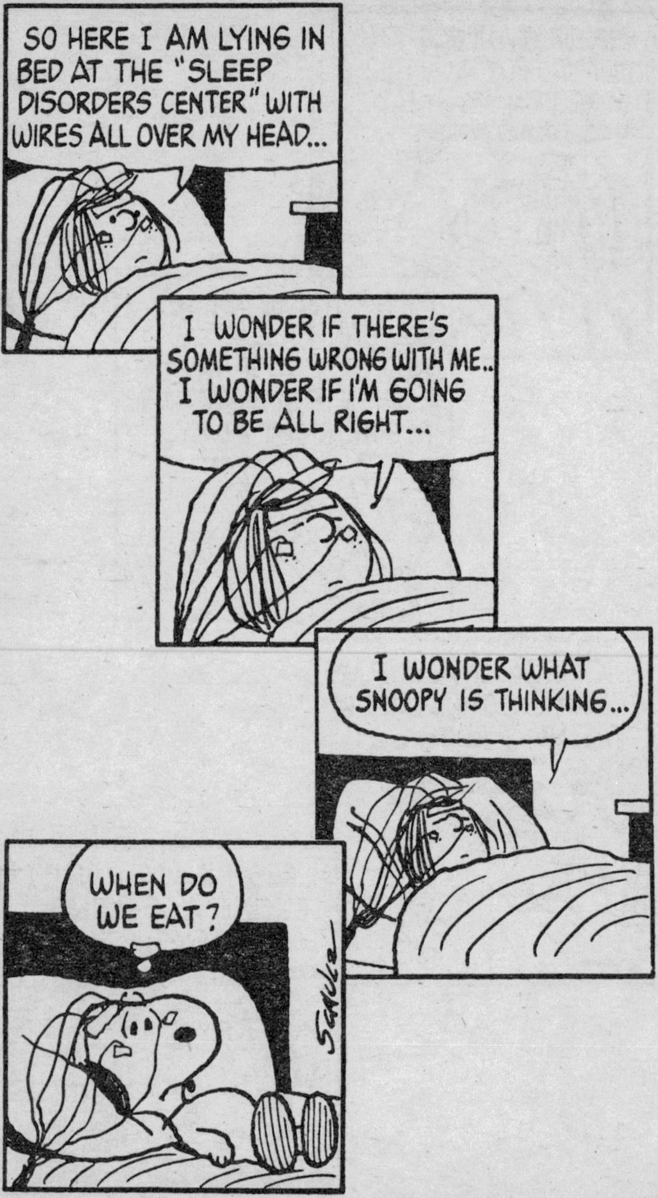
SO HERE I AM LYING IN BED AT THE "SLEEP DISORDERS CENTER" WITH WIRES ALL OVER MY HEAD...
I WONDER IF THERE'S SOMETHING WRONG WITH ME.. I WONDER IF I'M GOING TO BE ALL RIGHT...
I WONDER WHAT SNOOPY IS THINKING...
WHEN DO WE EAT?
SCHULZ

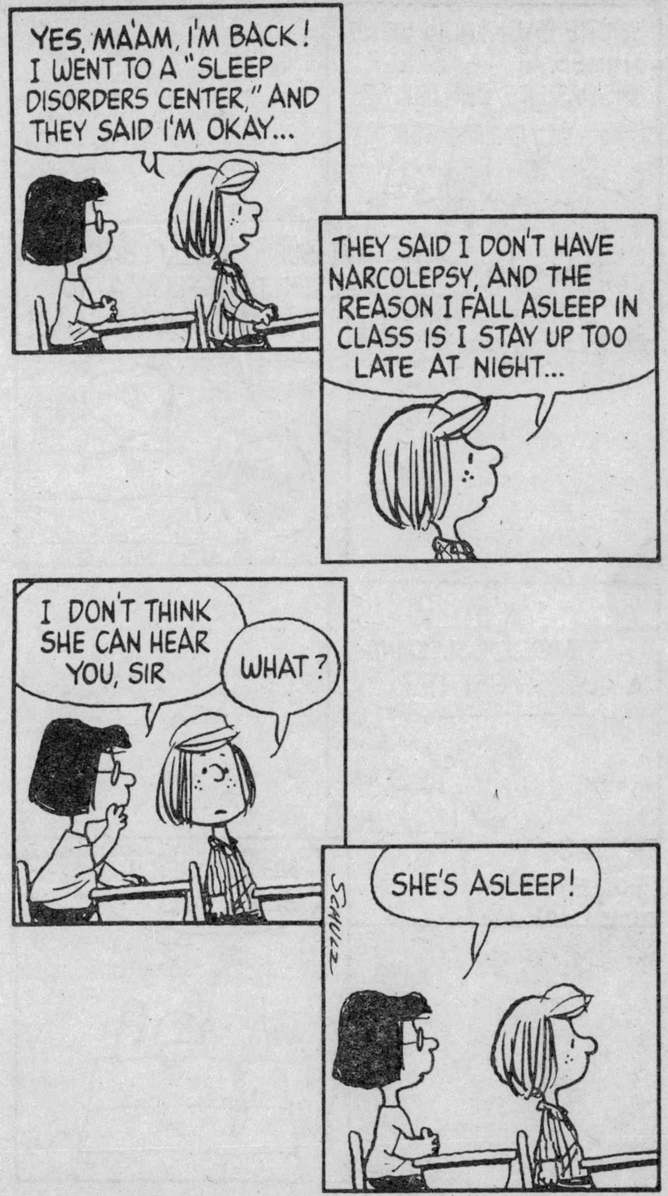
YES, MA'AM, I'M BACK! I WENT TO A "SLEEP DISORDERS CENTER," AND THEY SAID I'M OKAY...
THEY SAID I DON'T HAVE NARCOLEPSY, AND THE REASON I FALL ASLEEP IN CLASS IS I STAY UP TOO LATE AT NIGHT...
I DON'T THINK SHE CAN HEAR YOU, SIR
WHAT?
SHE'S ASLEEP!
SCHULZ

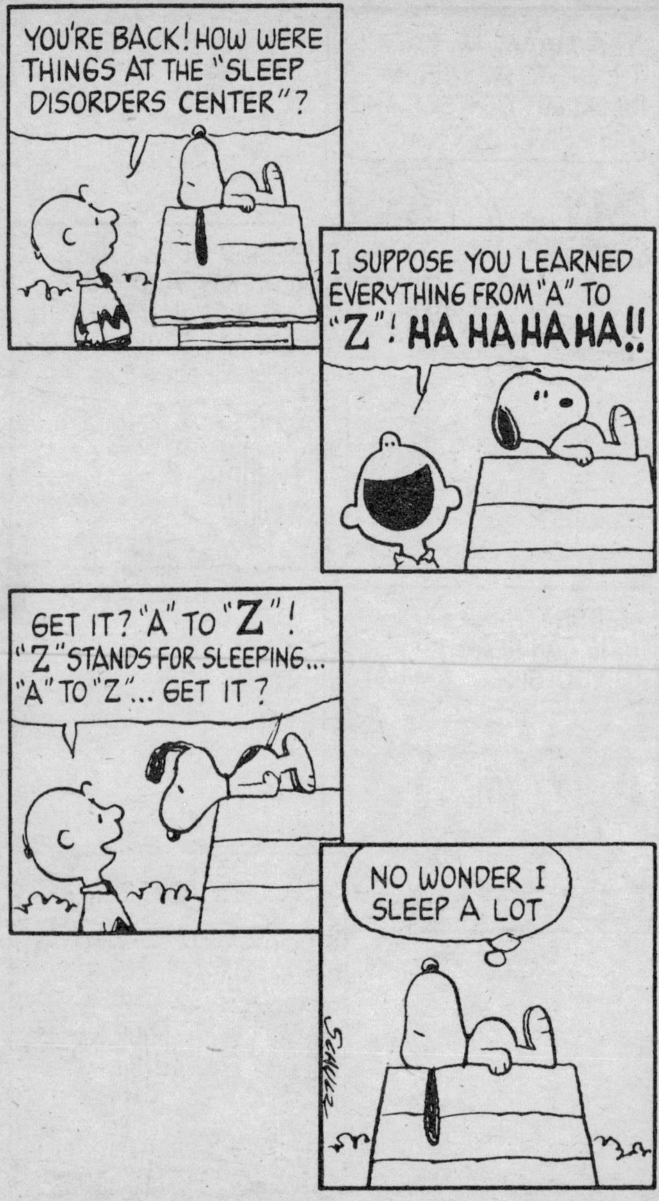
YOU'RE BACK! HOW WERE THINGS AT THE "SLEEP DISORDERS CENTER"?
I SUPPOSE YOU LEARNED EVERYTHING FROM "A" TO "Z"! HA HA HA HA!!
GET IT? "A" TO "Z"! "Z" STANDS FOR SLEEPING... "A" TO "Z"... GET IT?
NO WONDER I SLEEP A LOT
SCHULZ

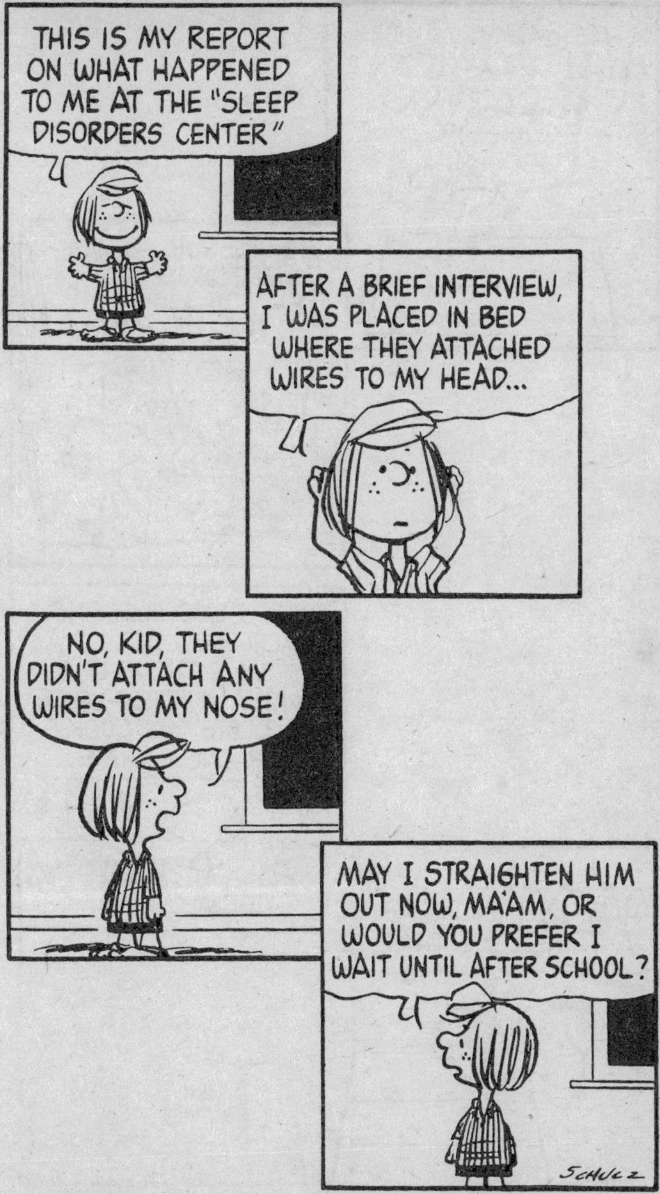
THIS IS MY REPORT ON WHAT HAPPENED TO ME AT THE "SLEEP DISORDERS CENTER"
AFTER A BRIEF INTERVIEW, I WAS PLACED IN BED WHERE THEY ATTACHED WIRES TO MY HEAD...
NO, KID, THEY DIDN'T ATTACH ANY WIRES TO MY NOSE!
MAY I STRAIGHTEN HIM OUT NOW, MA'AM, OR WOULD YOU PREFER I WAIT UNTIL AFTER SCHOOL?
SCHULZ

NOPE, YOU WERE WRONG

THERE I WAS, SLEEPING PEACEFULLY...ALL OF A SUDDEN, I THOUGHT I HEARD A HUNDRED-VOICE CHOCOLATE CHIP COOKIE CHOIR CALLING ME...

I WONDER HOW I COULD HAVE BEEN WRONG ABOUT A THING LIKE THAT..

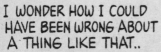

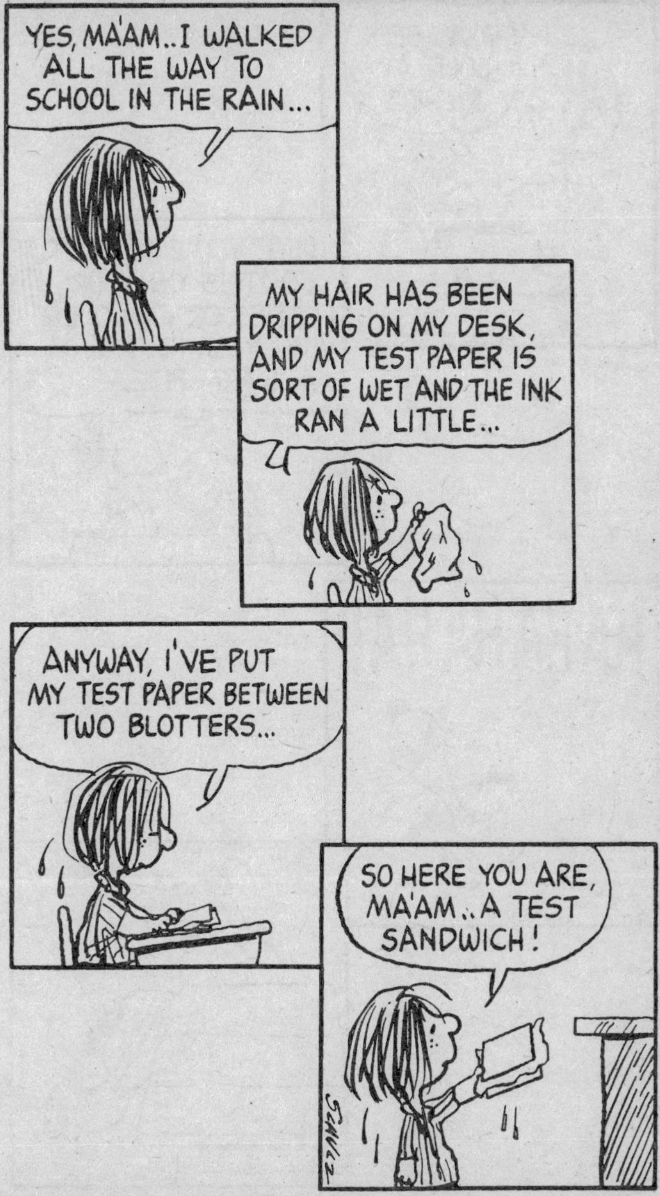
YES, MA'AM..I WALKED ALL THE WAY TO SCHOOL IN THE RAIN...
MY HAIR HAS BEEN DRIPPING ON MY DESK, AND MY TEST PAPER IS SORT OF WET AND THE INK RAN A LITTLE...
ANYWAY, I'VE PUT MY TEST PAPER BETWEEN TWO BLOTTERS...
SO HERE YOU ARE, MA'AM..A TEST SANDWICH!
SCHULZ

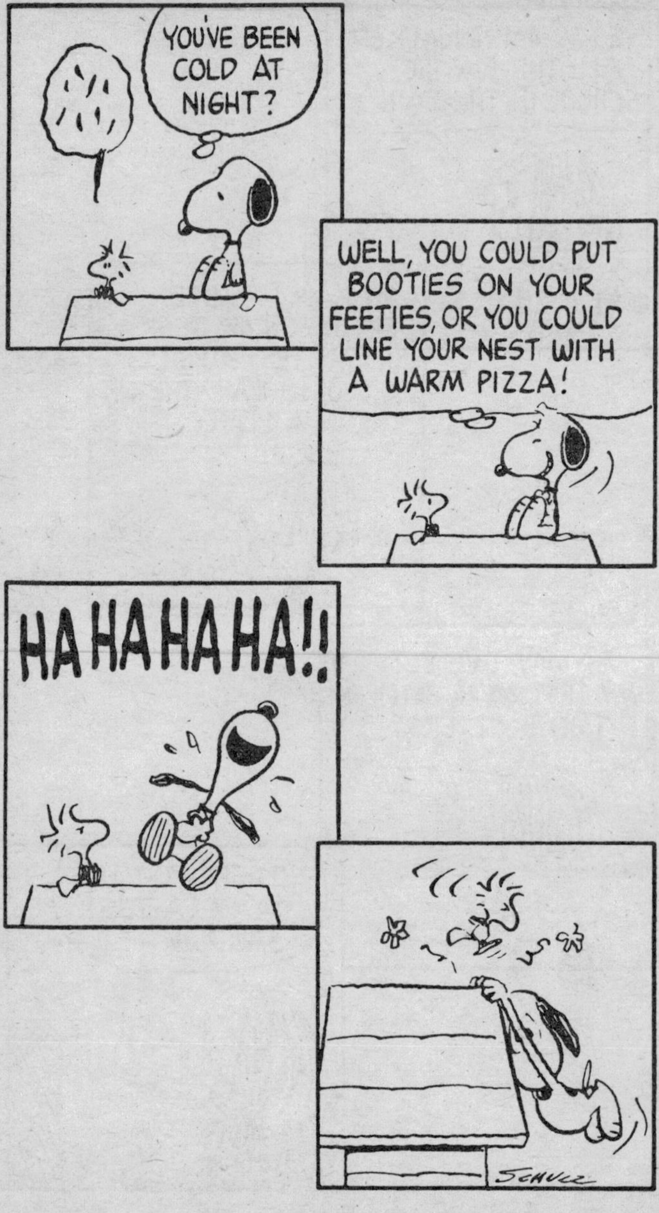
YOU'VE BEEN COLD AT NIGHT?
WELL, YOU COULD PUT BOOTIES ON YOUR FEETIES, OR YOU COULD LINE YOUR NEST WITH A WARM PIZZA!
HAHAHAHA!!
SCHULZ

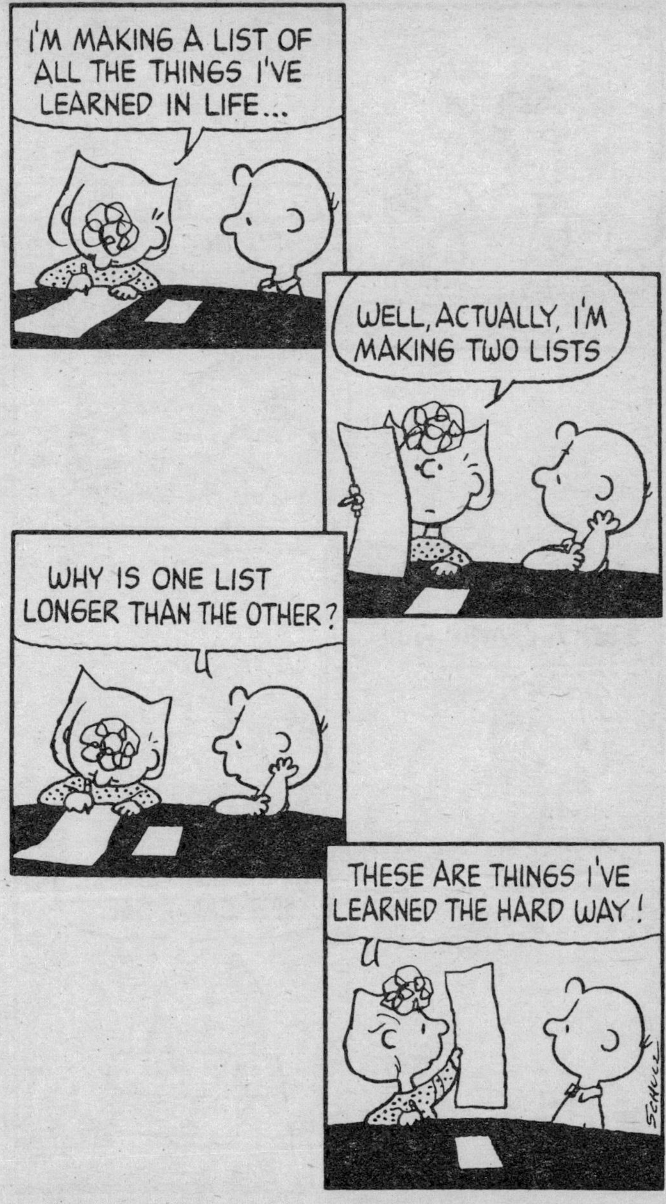
I'M MAKING A LIST OF ALL THE THINGS I'VE LEARNED IN LIFE...
WELL, ACTUALLY, I'M MAKING TWO LISTS
WHY IS ONE LIST LONGER THAN THE OTHER?
THESE ARE THINGS I'VE LEARNED THE HARD WAY!
SCHULZ

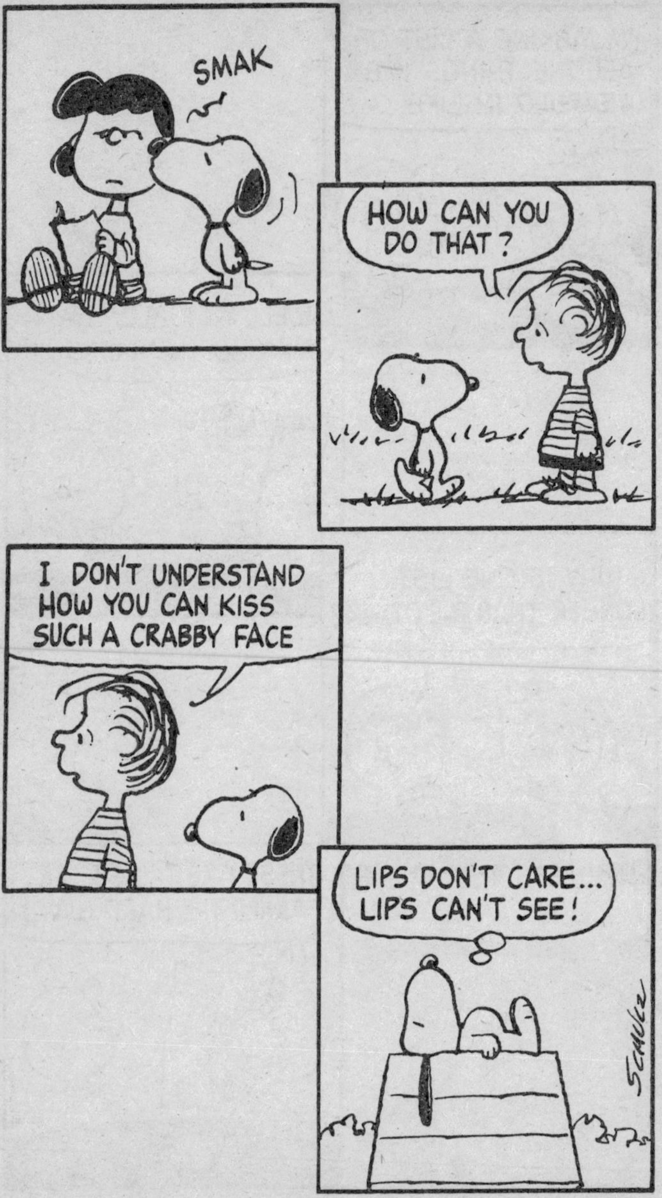
SMAK
HOW CAN YOU DO THAT?
I DON'T UNDERSTAND HOW YOU CAN KISS SUCH A CRABBY FACE
LIPS DON'T CARE... LIPS CAN'T SEE!
SCHULZ

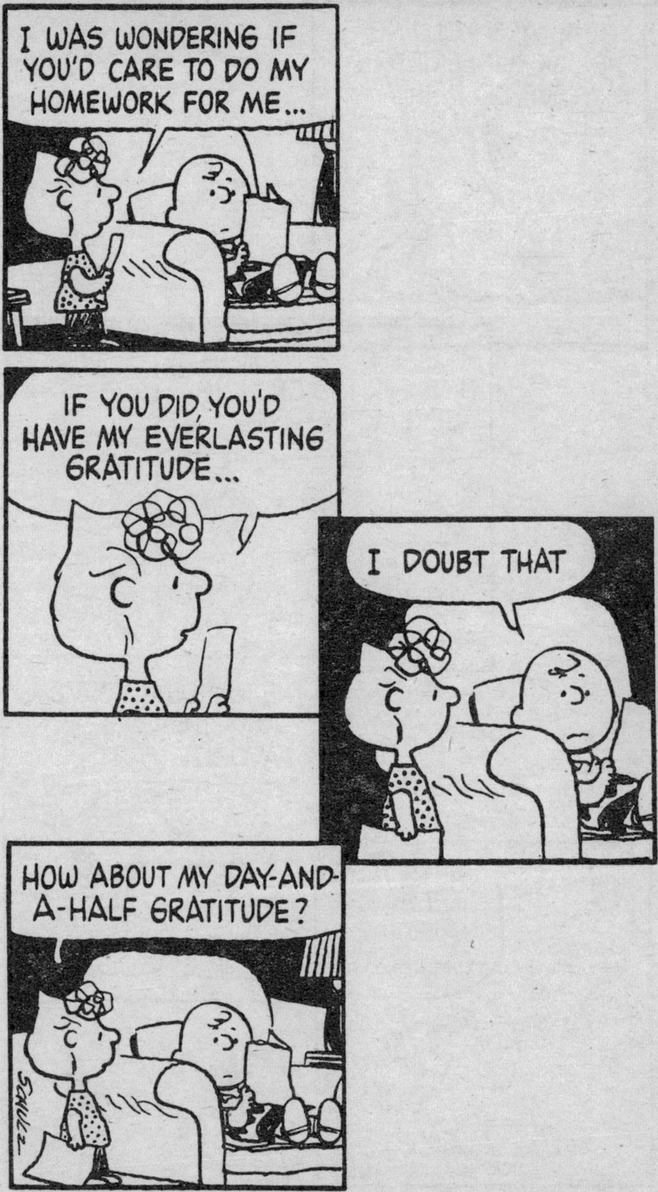
I WAS WONDERING IF YOU'D CARE TO DO MY HOMEWORK FOR ME...
IF YOU DID, YOU'D HAVE MY EVERLASTING GRATITUDE...
I DOUBT THAT
HOW ABOUT MY DAY-AND-A-HALF GRATITUDE?
SCHULZ

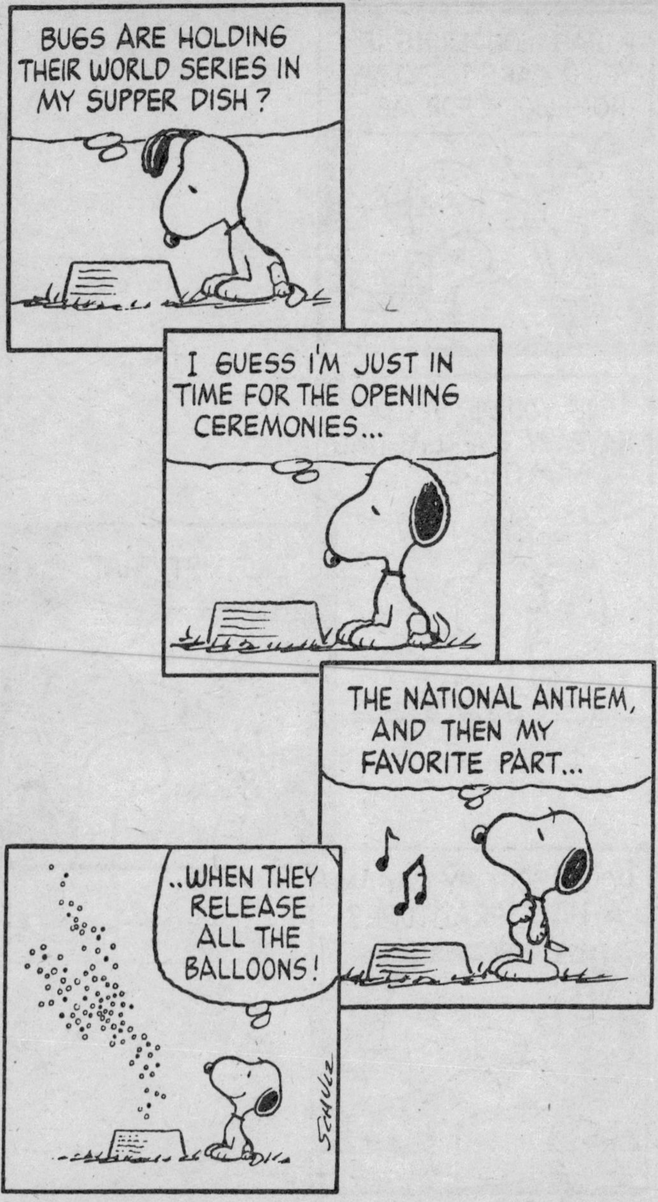
BUGS ARE HOLDING THEIR WORLD SERIES IN MY SUPPER DISH?
I GUESS I'M JUST IN TIME FOR THE OPENING CEREMONIES...
THE NATIONAL ANTHEM, AND THEN MY FAVORITE PART...
..WHEN THEY RELEASE ALL THE BALLOONS!
SCHULZ

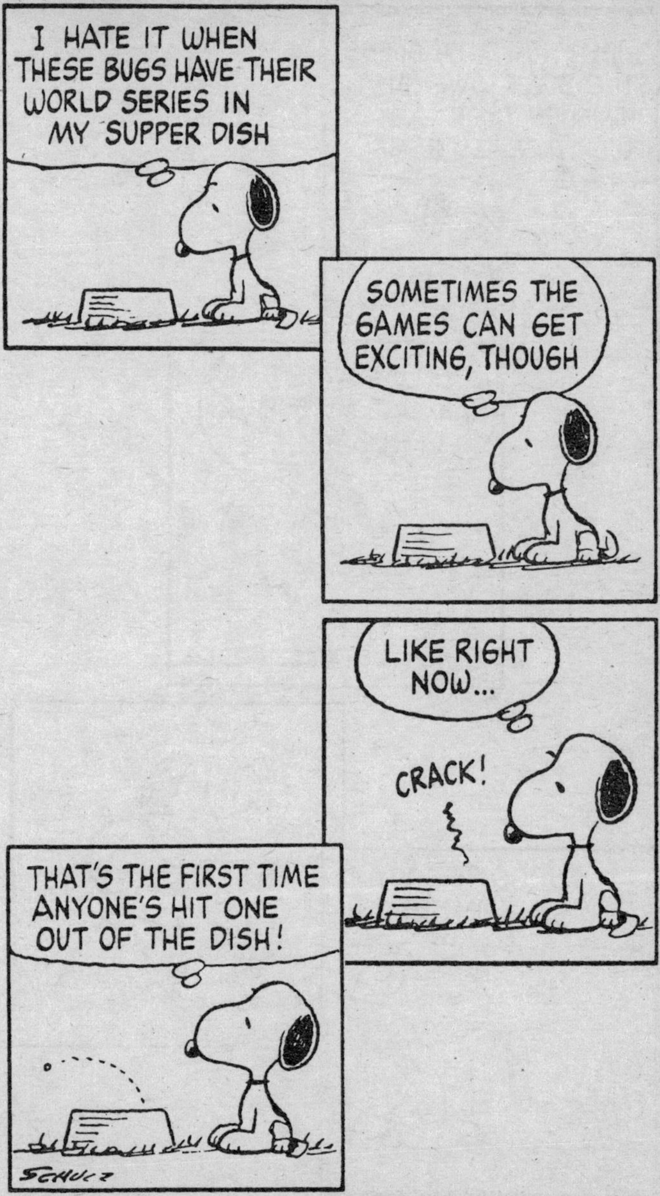
I HATE IT WHEN THESE BUGS HAVE THEIR WORLD SERIES IN MY SUPPER DISH
SOMETIMES THE GAMES CAN GET EXCITING, THOUGH
LIKE RIGHT NOW...
CRACK!
THAT'S THE FIRST TIME ANYONE'S HIT ONE OUT OF THE DISH!
SCHULZ

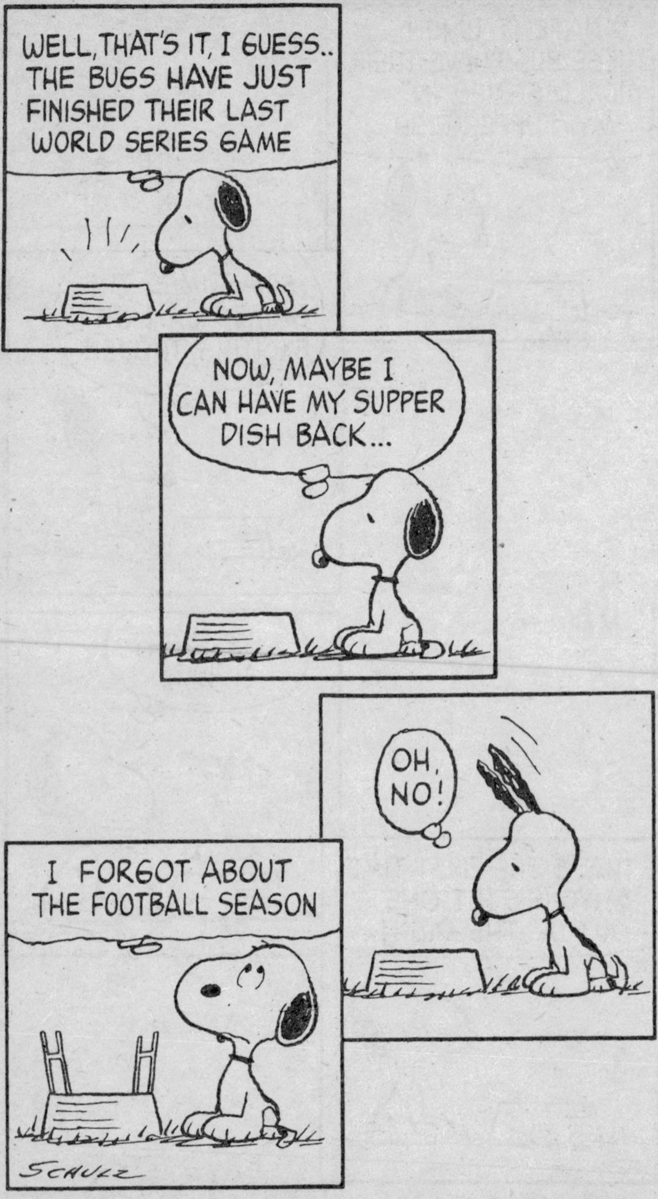
WELL, THAT'S IT, I GUESS.. THE BUGS HAVE JUST FINISHED THEIR LAST WORLD SERIES GAME
NOW, MAYBE I CAN HAVE MY SUPPER DISH BACK...
OH, NO!
I FORGOT ABOUT THE FOOTBALL SEASON
SCHULZ

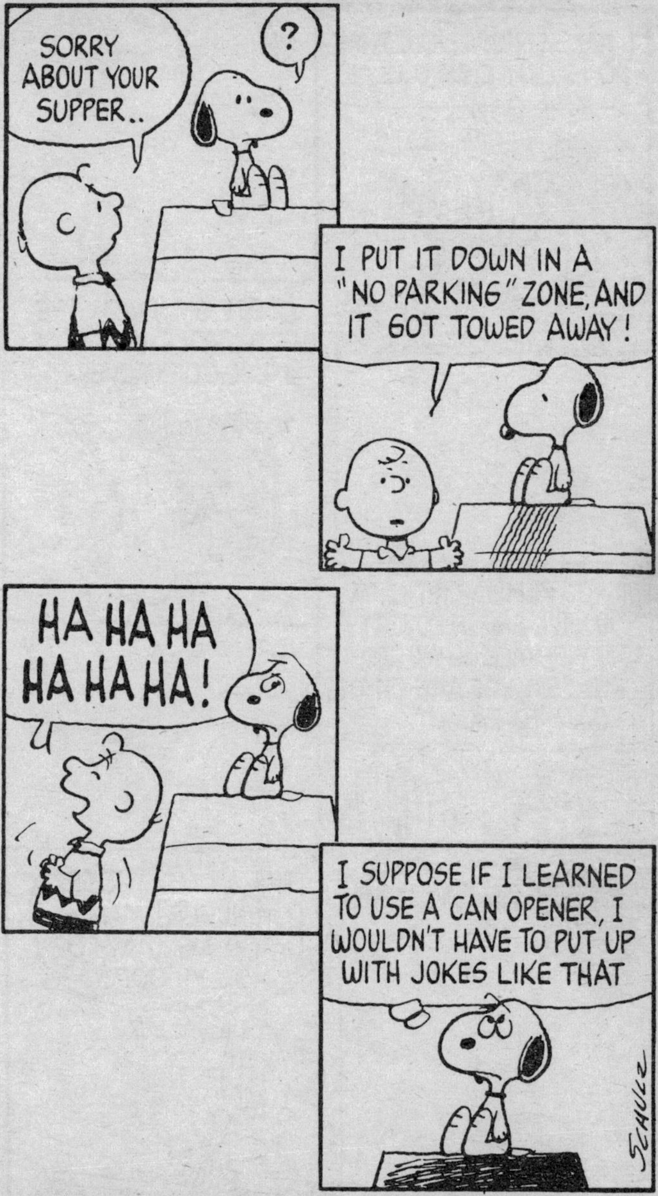
SORRY ABOUT YOUR SUPPER..
?
I PUT IT DOWN IN A "NO PARKING" ZONE, AND IT GOT TOWED AWAY!
HA HA HA HA HA HA!
I SUPPOSE IF I LEARNED TO USE A CAN OPENER, I WOULDN'T HAVE TO PUT UP WITH JOKES LIKE THAT
SCHULZ

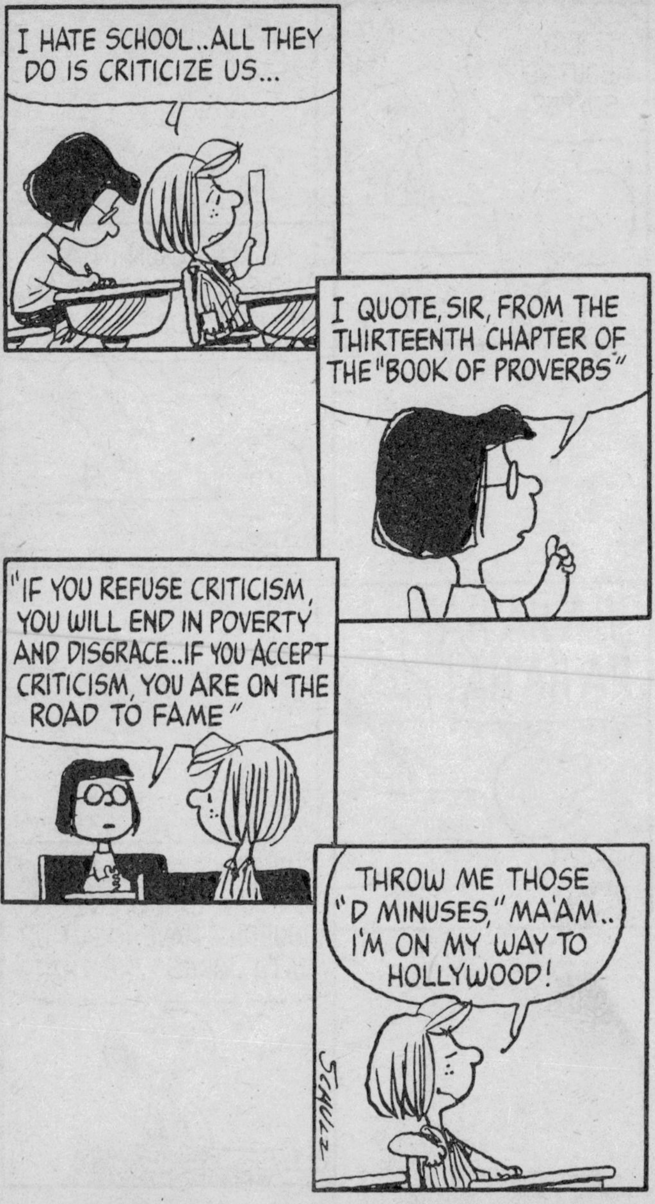
I HATE SCHOOL..ALL THEY DO IS CRITICIZE US...
I QUOTE, SIR, FROM THE THIRTEENTH CHAPTER OF THE "BOOK OF PROVERBS"
"IF YOU REFUSE CRITICISM, YOU WILL END IN POVERTY AND DISGRACE..IF YOU ACCEPT CRITICISM, YOU ARE ON THE ROAD TO FAME"
THROW ME THOSE "D MINUSES," MA'AM.. I'M ON MY WAY TO HOLLYWOOD!
SCHULZ

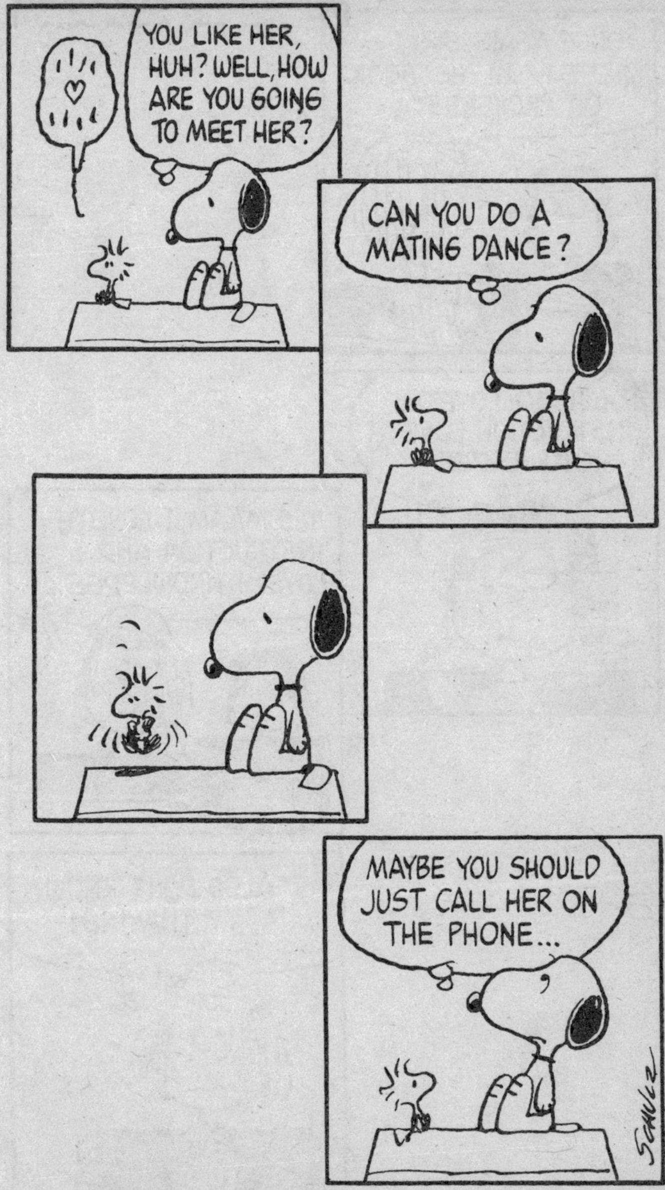
YOU LIKE HER, HUH? WELL, HOW ARE YOU GOING TO MEET HER?
CAN YOU DO A MATING DANCE?
MAYBE YOU SHOULD JUST CALL HER ON THE PHONE...
SCHULZ

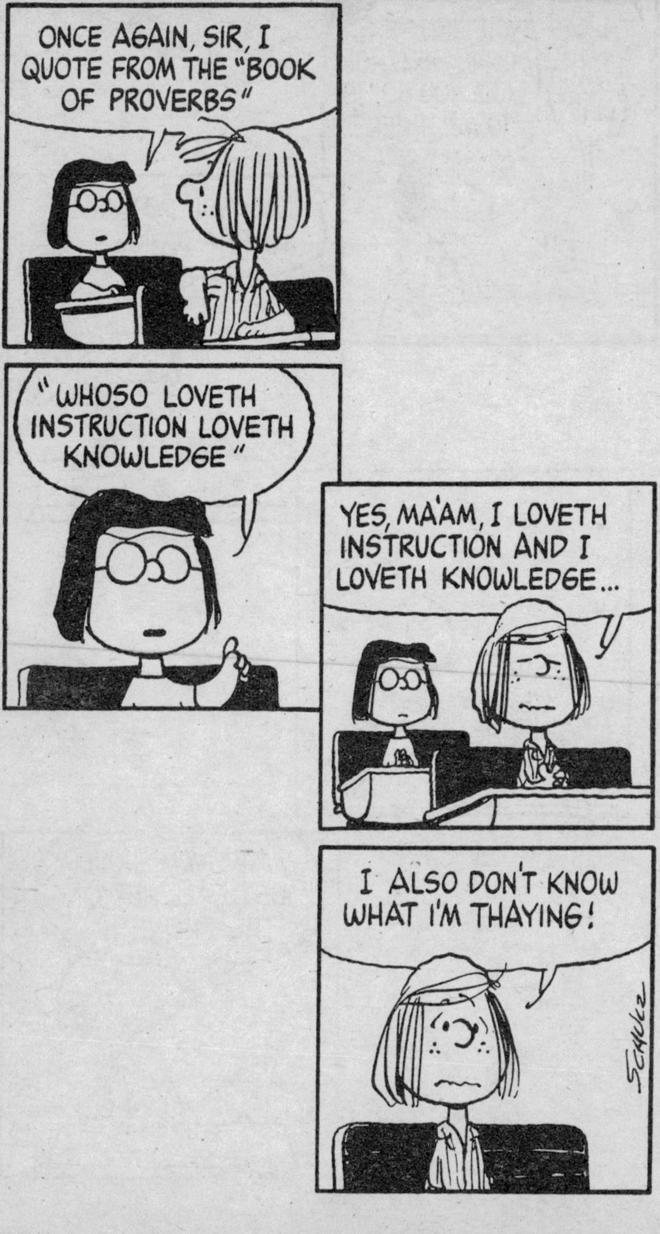
ONCE AGAIN, SIR, I QUOTE FROM THE "BOOK OF PROVERBS"
"WHOSO LOVETH INSTRUCTION LOVETH KNOWLEDGE"
YES, MA'AM, I LOVETH INSTRUCTION AND I LOVETH KNOWLEDGE...
I ALSO DON'T KNOW WHAT I'M THAYING!
SCHULZ

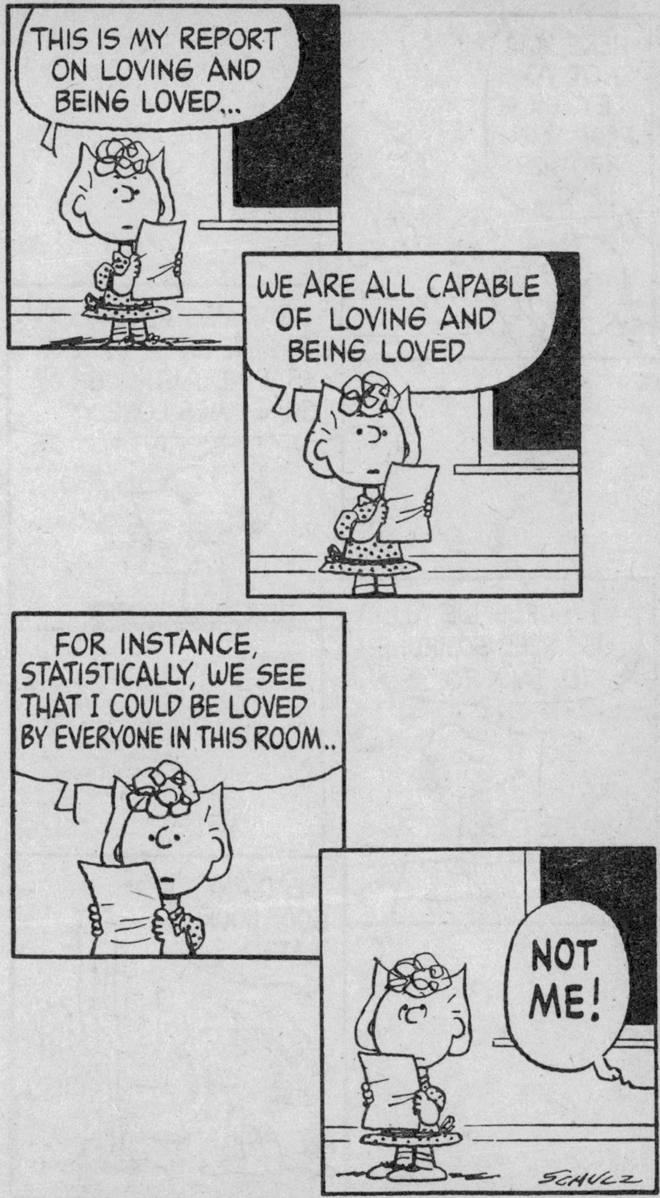
THIS IS MY REPORT ON LOVING AND BEING LOVED...
WE ARE ALL CAPABLE OF LOVING AND BEING LOVED
FOR INSTANCE, STATISTICALLY, WE SEE THAT I COULD BE LOVED BY EVERYONE IN THIS ROOM..
NOT ME!
SCHULZ

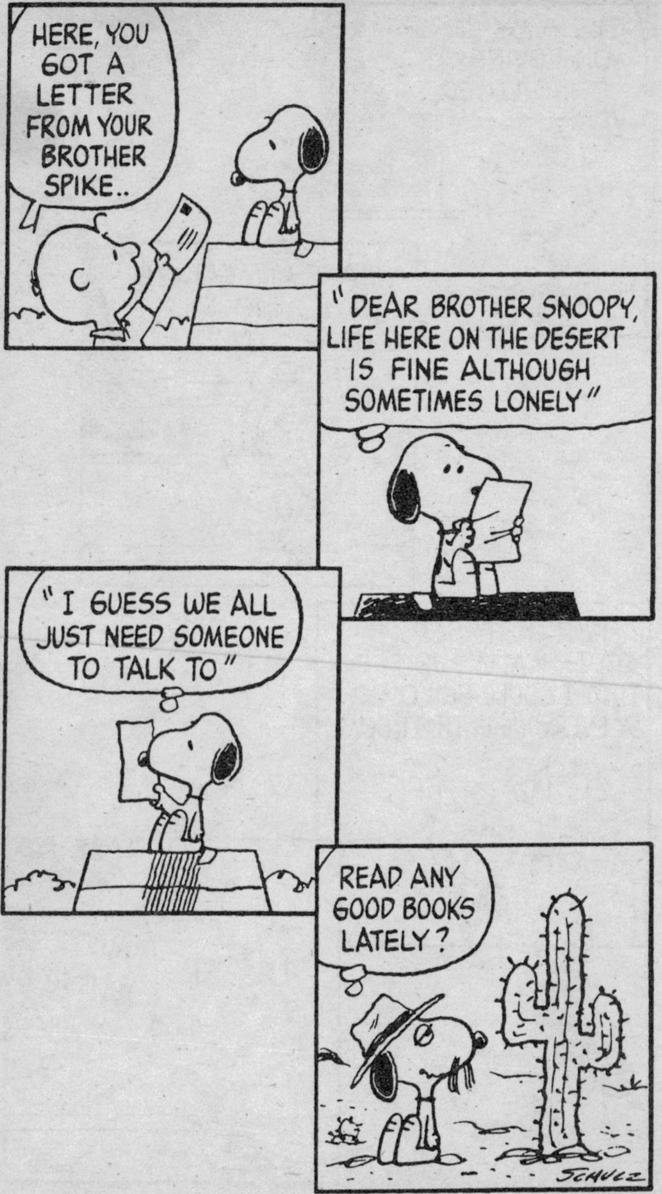
HERE, YOU GOT A LETTER FROM YOUR BROTHER SPIKE..
"DEAR BROTHER SNOOPY, LIFE HERE ON THE DESERT IS FINE ALTHOUGH SOMETIMES LONELY"
"I GUESS WE ALL JUST NEED SOMEONE TO TALK TO"
READ ANY GOOD BOOKS LATELY?
SCHULZ

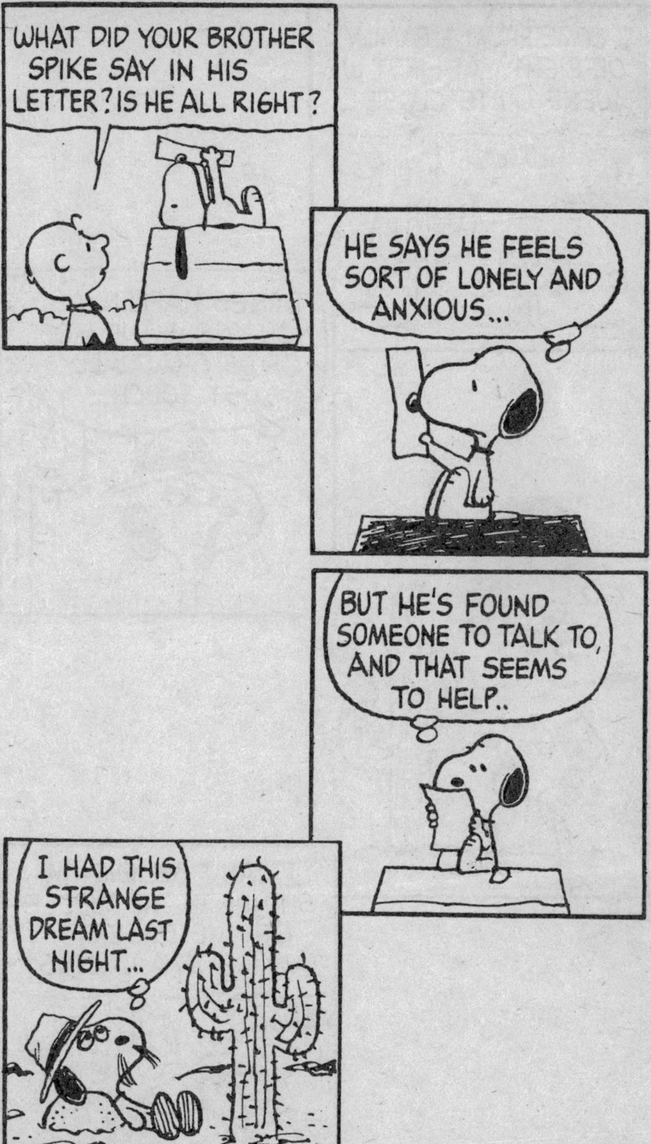
WHAT DID YOUR BROTHER SPIKE SAY IN HIS LETTER? IS HE ALL RIGHT?
HE SAYS HE FEELS SORT OF LONELY AND ANXIOUS...
BUT HE'S FOUND SOMEONE TO TALK TO, AND THAT SEEMS TO HELP..
I HAD THIS STRANGE DREAM LAST NIGHT...
SCHULZ

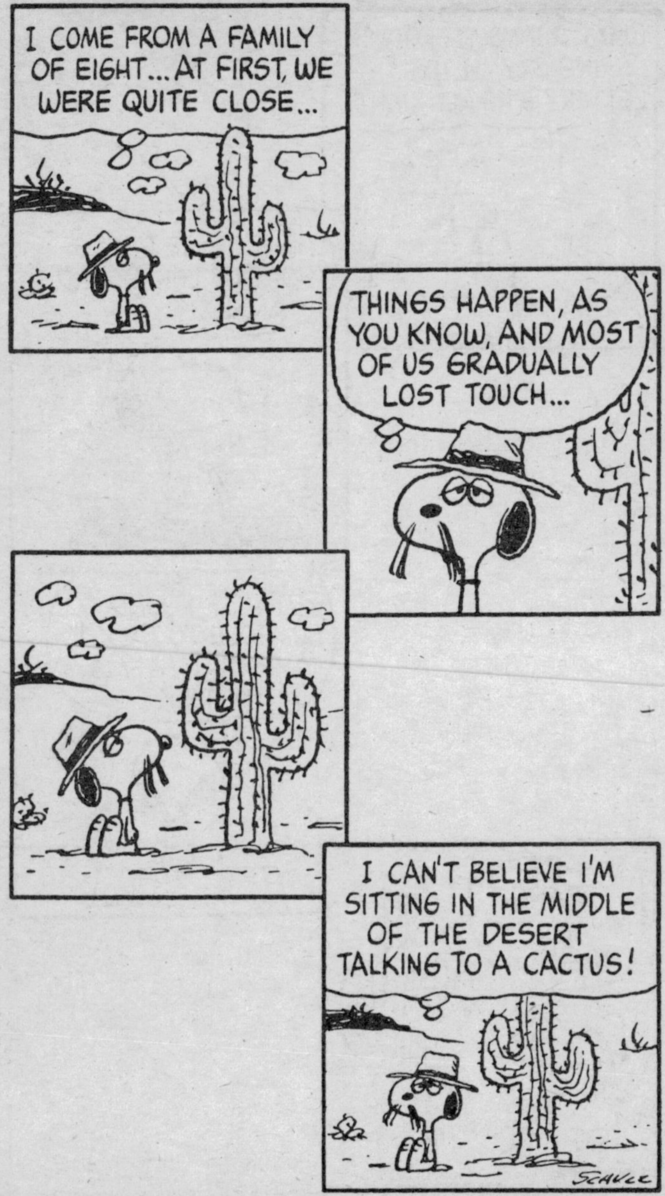
I COME FROM A FAMILY OF EIGHT... AT FIRST, WE WERE QUITE CLOSE...
THINGS HAPPEN, AS YOU KNOW, AND MOST OF US GRADUALLY LOST TOUCH...
I CAN'T BELIEVE I'M SITTING IN THE MIDDLE OF THE DESERT TALKING TO A CACTUS!
SCHULZ

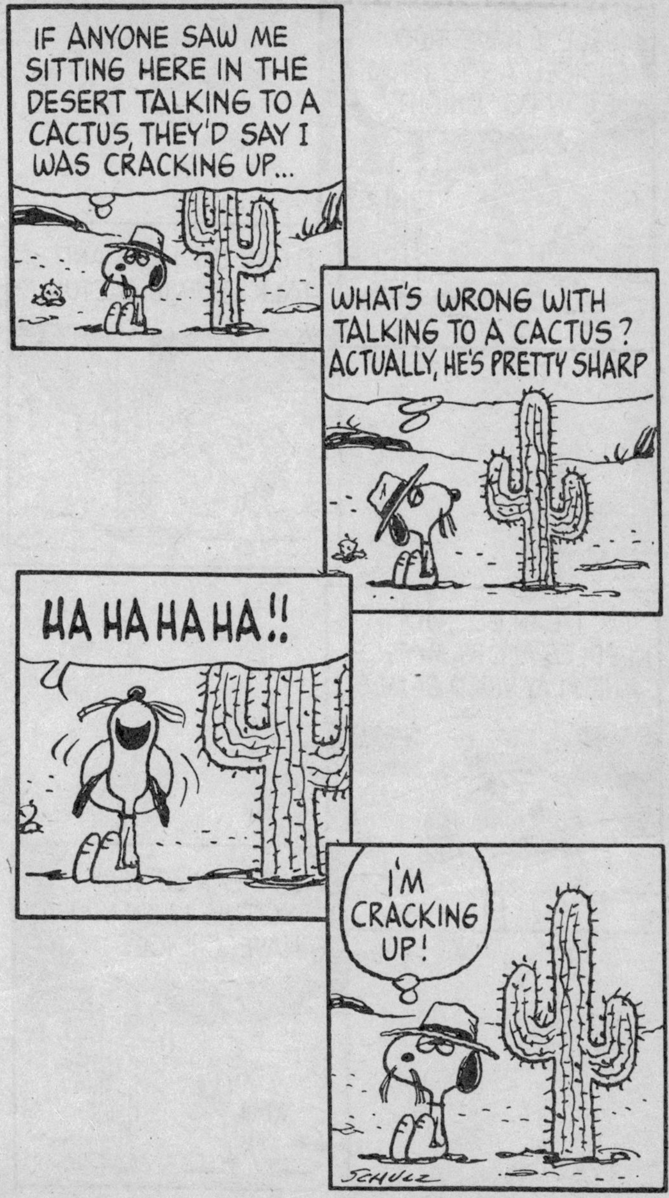
IF ANYONE SAW ME SITTING HERE IN THE DESERT TALKING TO A CACTUS, THEY'D SAY I WAS CRACKING UP...
WHAT'S WRONG WITH TALKING TO A CACTUS? ACTUALLY, HE'S PRETTY SHARP
HA HA HA HA HA!!
I'M CRACKING UP!
SCHULZ

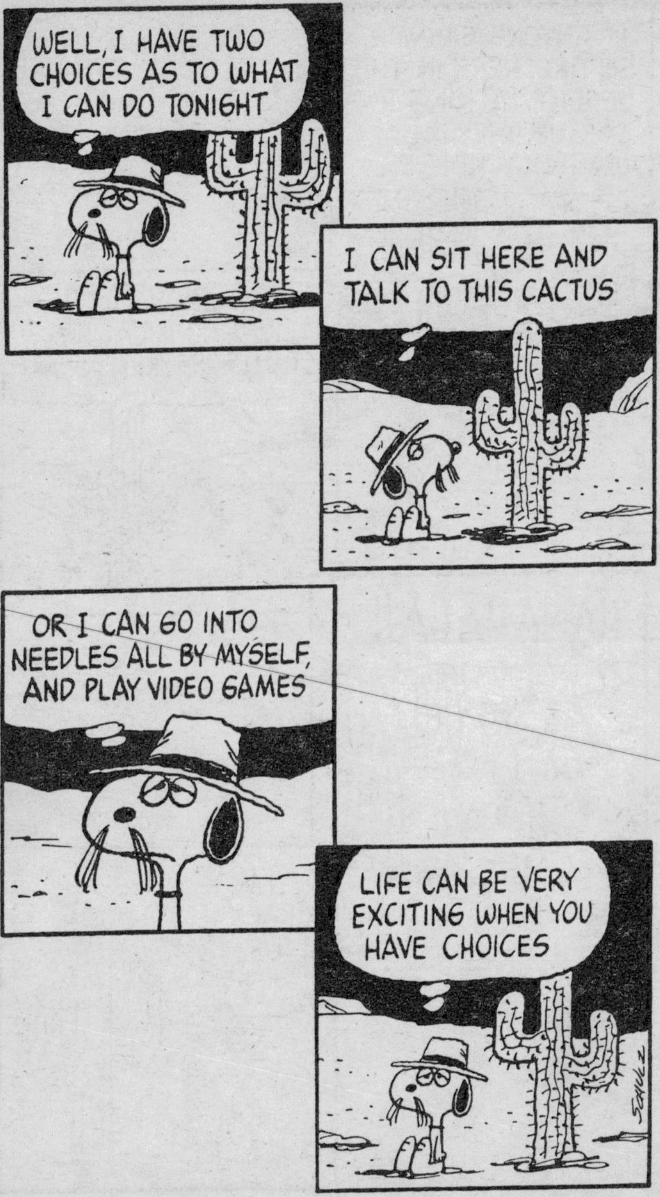
WELL, I HAVE TWO CHOICES AS TO WHAT I CAN DO TONIGHT
I CAN SIT HERE AND TALK TO THIS CACTUS
OR I CAN GO INTO NEEDLES ALL BY MYSELF, AND PLAY VIDEO GAMES
LIFE CAN BE VERY EXCITING WHEN YOU HAVE CHOICES
SCHULZ

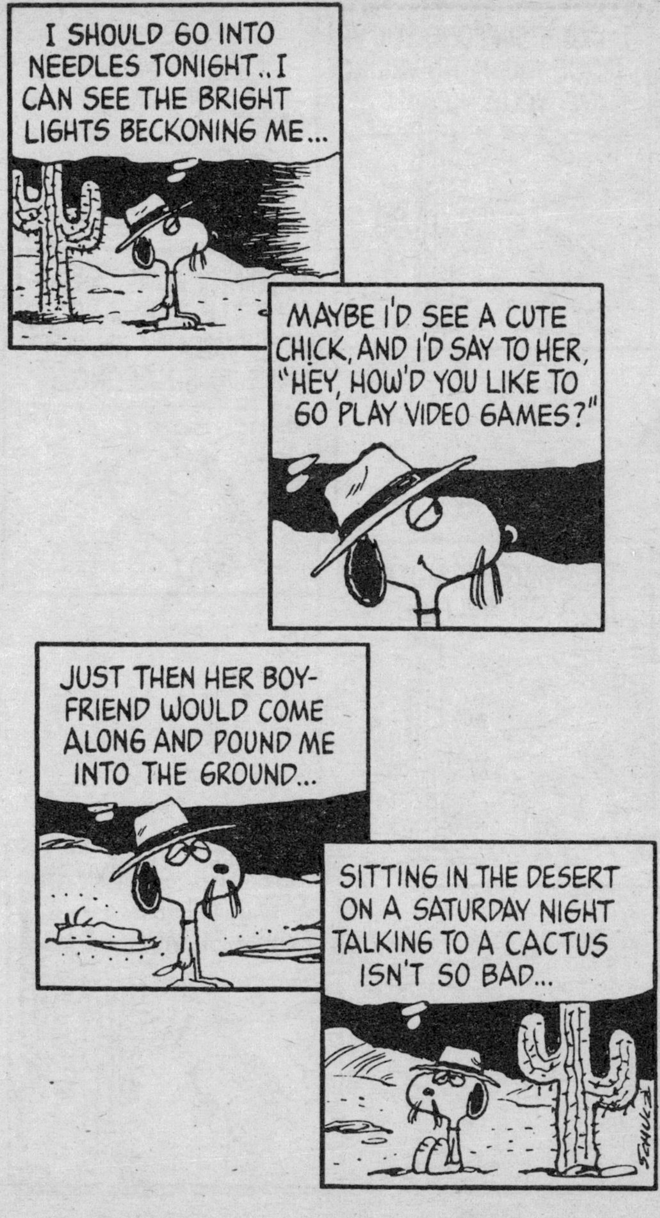
I SHOULD GO INTO NEEDLES TONIGHT.. I CAN SEE THE BRIGHT LIGHTS BECKONING ME...
MAYBE I'D SEE A CUTE CHICK, AND I'D SAY TO HER, "HEY, HOW'D YOU LIKE TO GO PLAY VIDEO GAMES?"
JUST THEN HER BOY-FRIEND WOULD COME ALONG AND POUND ME INTO THE GROUND...
SITTING IN THE DESERT ON A SATURDAY NIGHT TALKING TO A CACTUS ISN'T SO BAD...
SCHULZ

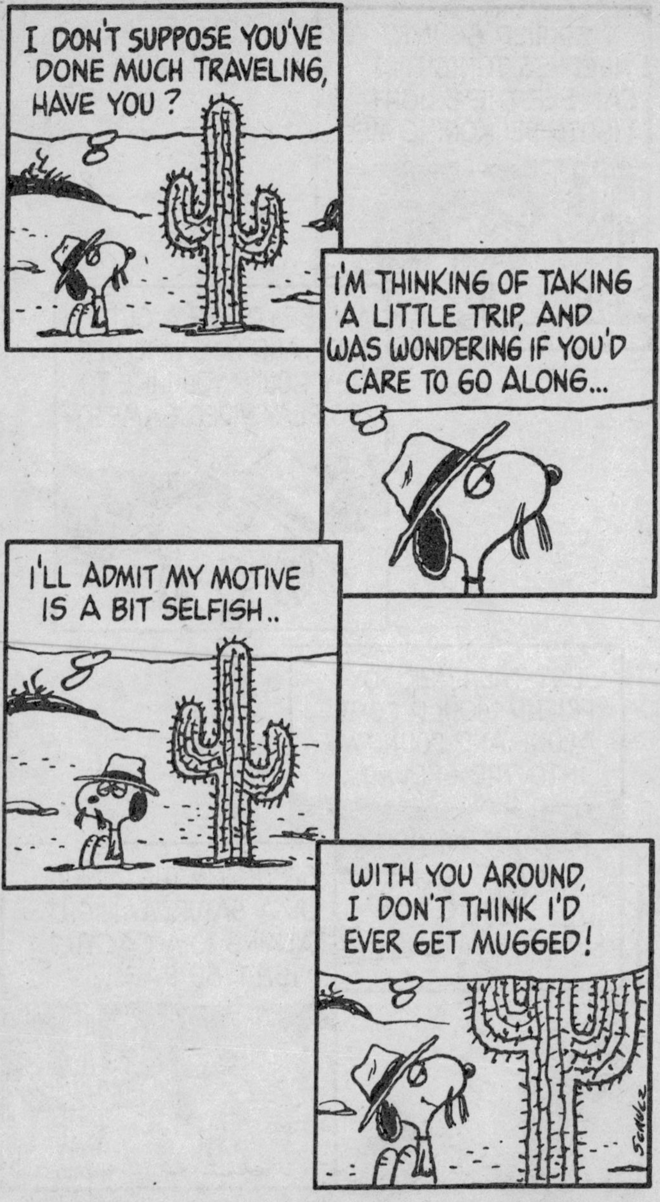

I DON'T SUPPOSE YOU'VE DONE MUCH TRAVELING, HAVE YOU ?
I'M THINKING OF TAKING A LITTLE TRIP, AND WAS WONDERING IF YOU'D CARE TO GO ALONG...
I'LL ADMIT MY MOTIVE IS A BIT SELFISH..
WITH YOU AROUND, I DON'T THINK I'D EVER GET MUGGED!
SCHULZ

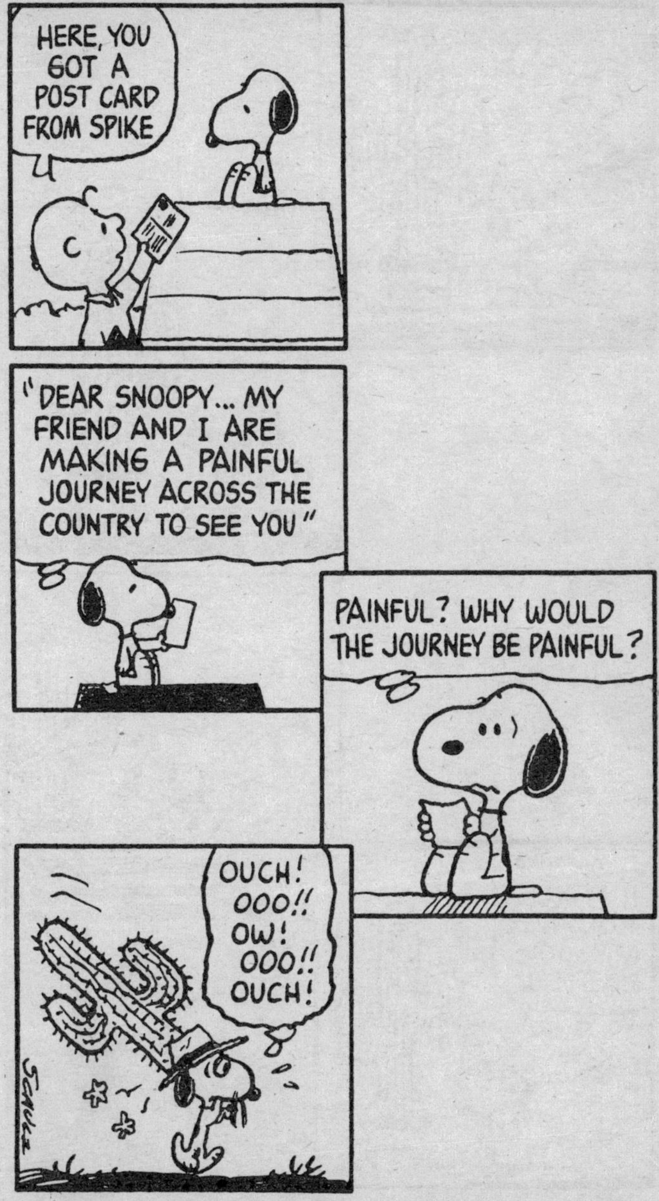
HERE, YOU GOT A POST CARD FROM SPIKE
"DEAR SNOOPY... MY FRIEND AND I ARE MAKING A PAINFUL JOURNEY ACROSS THE COUNTRY TO SEE YOU"
PAINFUL? WHY WOULD THE JOURNEY BE PAINFUL?
OUCH! OOO!! OW! OOO!! OUCH!
SCHULZ

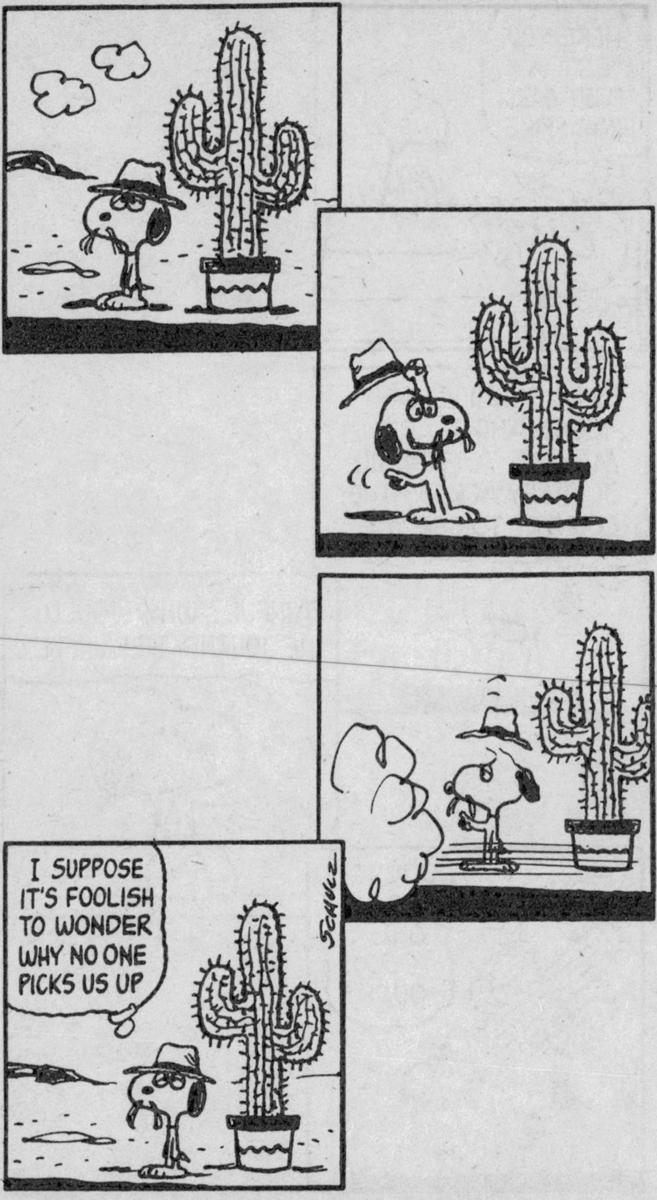
SCHULZ
I SUPPOSE IT'S FOOLISH TO WONDER WHY NO ONE PICKS US UP

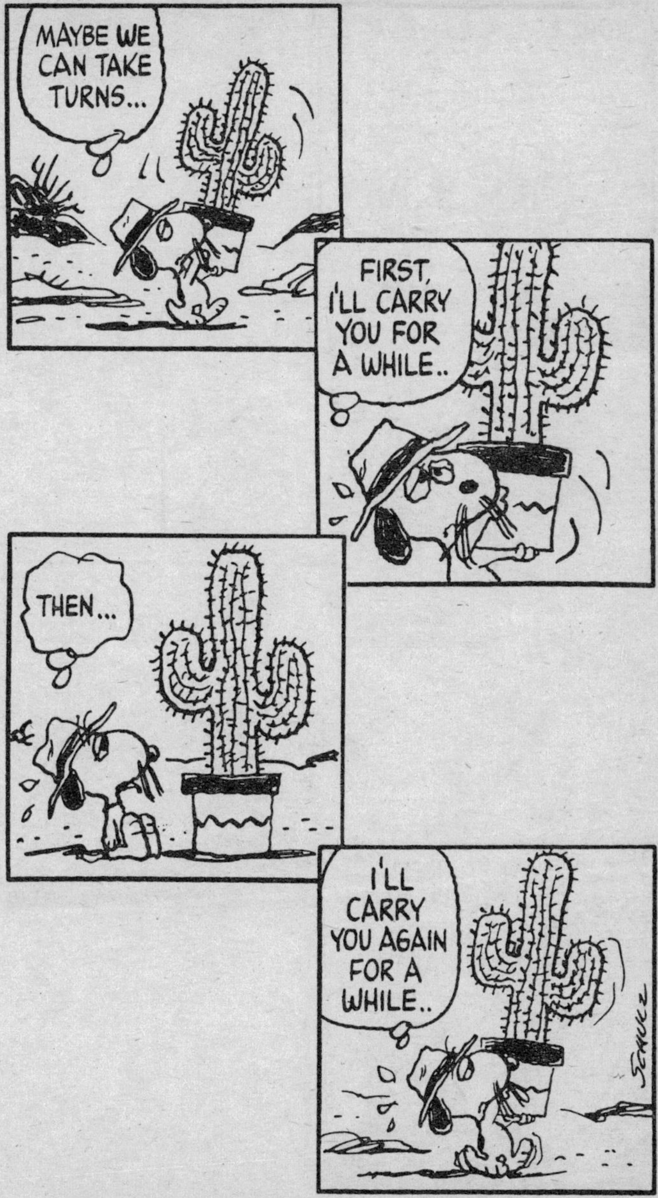
MAYBE WE CAN TAKE TURNS...
FIRST, I'LL CARRY YOU FOR A WHILE..
THEN...
I'LL CARRY YOU AGAIN FOR A WHILE..
SCHULZ

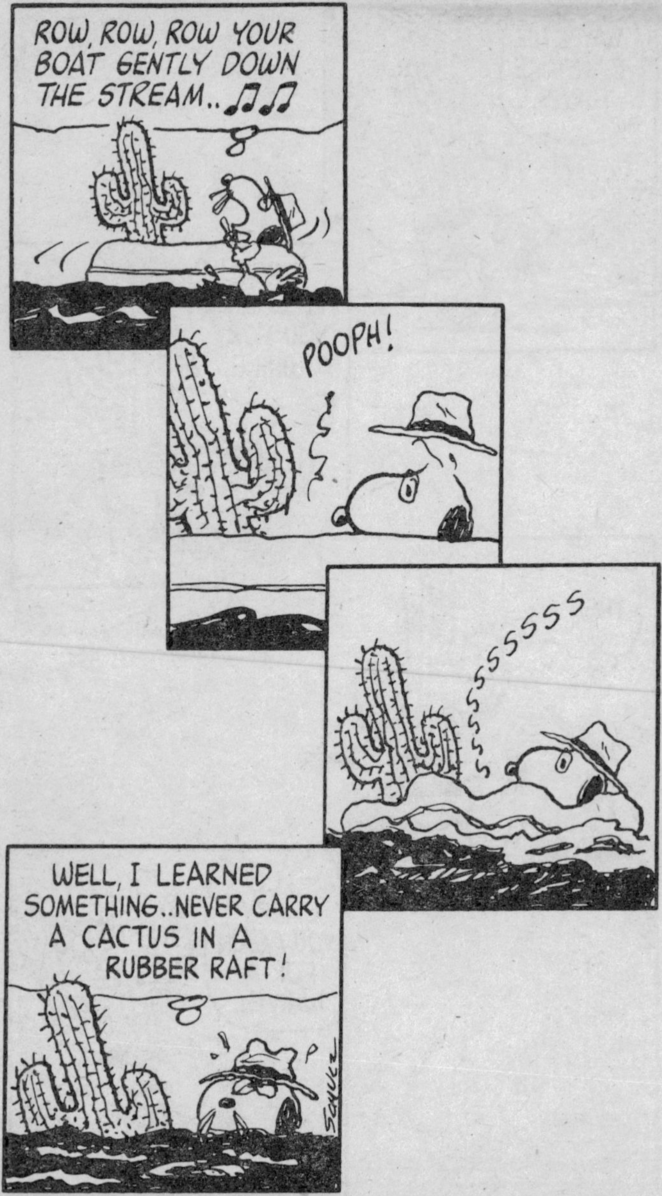
ROW, ROW, ROW YOUR BOAT GENTLY DOWN THE STREAM..
POOPH!
SSSSSSSSSSSSS
WELL, I LEARNED SOMETHING..NEVER CARRY A CACTUS IN A RUBBER RAFT!
SCHULZ

Motel
VACANCY
NO?!!
OKAY, THEN WE'LL SLEEP OUTSIDE
IF YOUR ARM GETS TIRED, LET ME KNOW

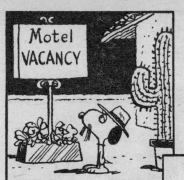

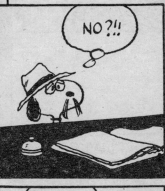

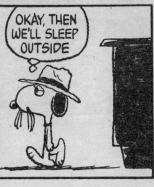

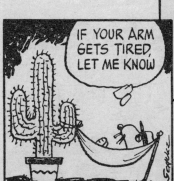

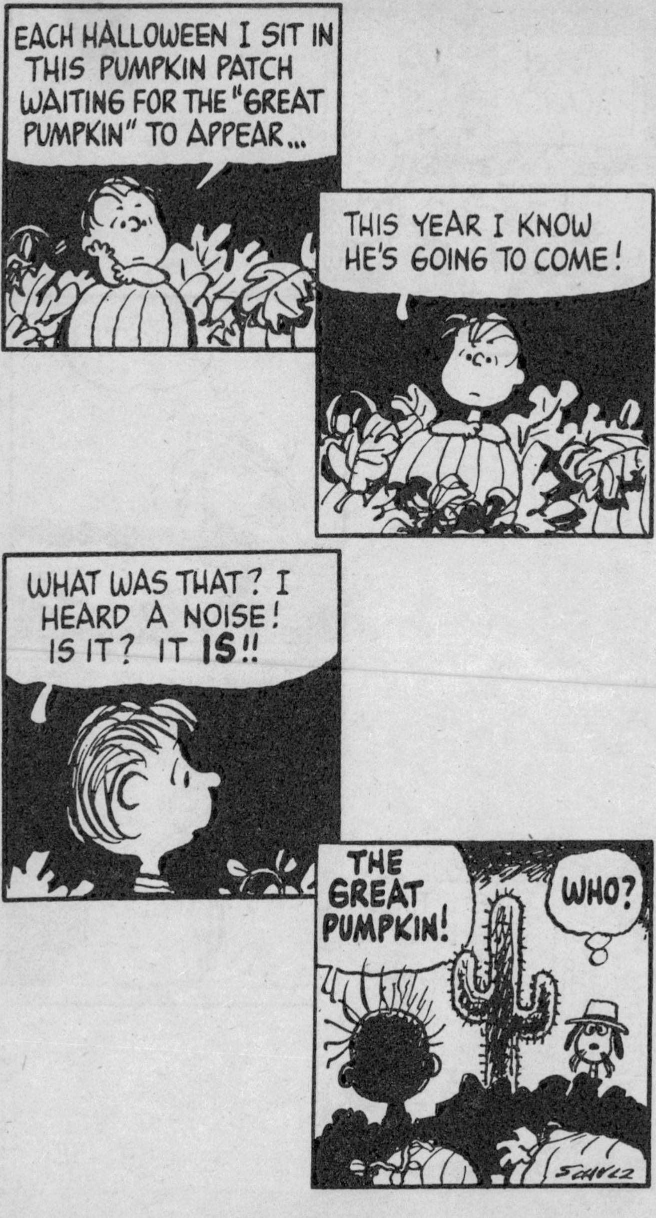
EACH HALLOWEEN I SIT IN THIS PUMPKIN PATCH WAITING FOR THE "GREAT PUMPKIN" TO APPEAR...
THIS YEAR I KNOW HE'S GOING TO COME!
WHAT WAS THAT? I HEARD A NOISE! IS IT? IT IS!!
THE GREAT PUMPKIN!
WHO?
SCHULZ

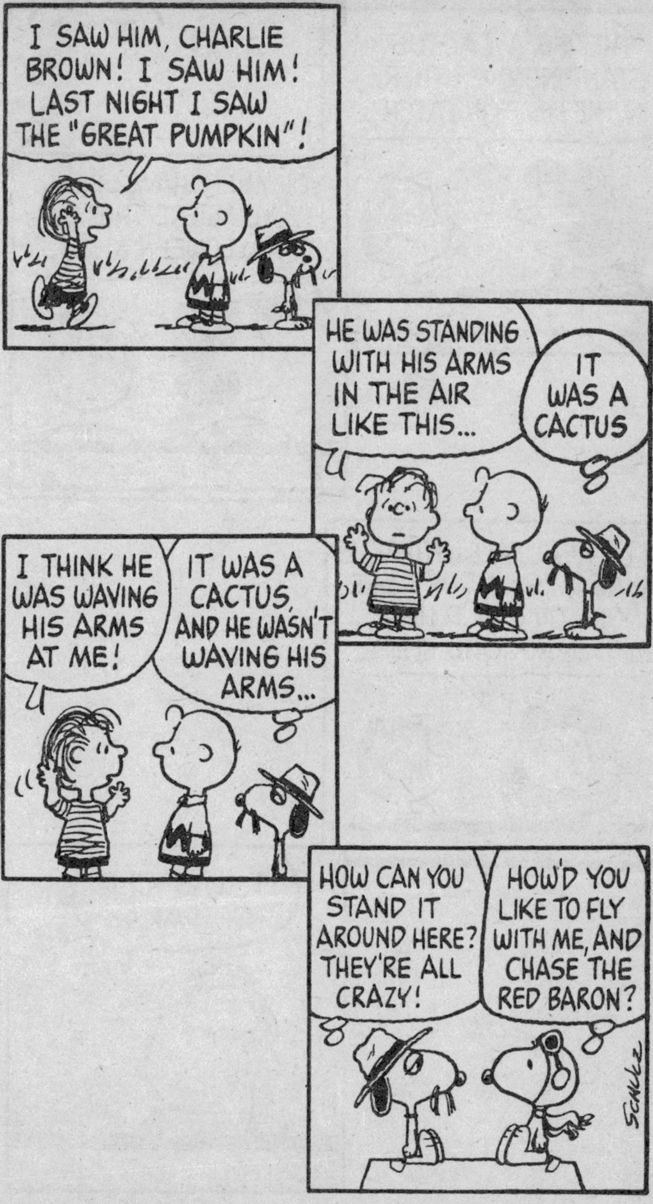
I SAW HIM, CHARLIE BROWN! I SAW HIM! LAST NIGHT I SAW THE "GREAT PUMPKIN"!
HE WAS STANDING WITH HIS ARMS IN THE AIR LIKE THIS...
IT WAS A CACTUS
I THINK HE WAS WAVING HIS ARMS AT ME!
IT WAS A CACTUS, AND HE WASN'T WAVING HIS ARMS...
HOW CAN YOU STAND IT AROUND HERE? THEY'RE ALL CRAZY!
HOW'D YOU LIKE TO FLY WITH ME, AND CHASE THE RED BARON?
SCHULZ

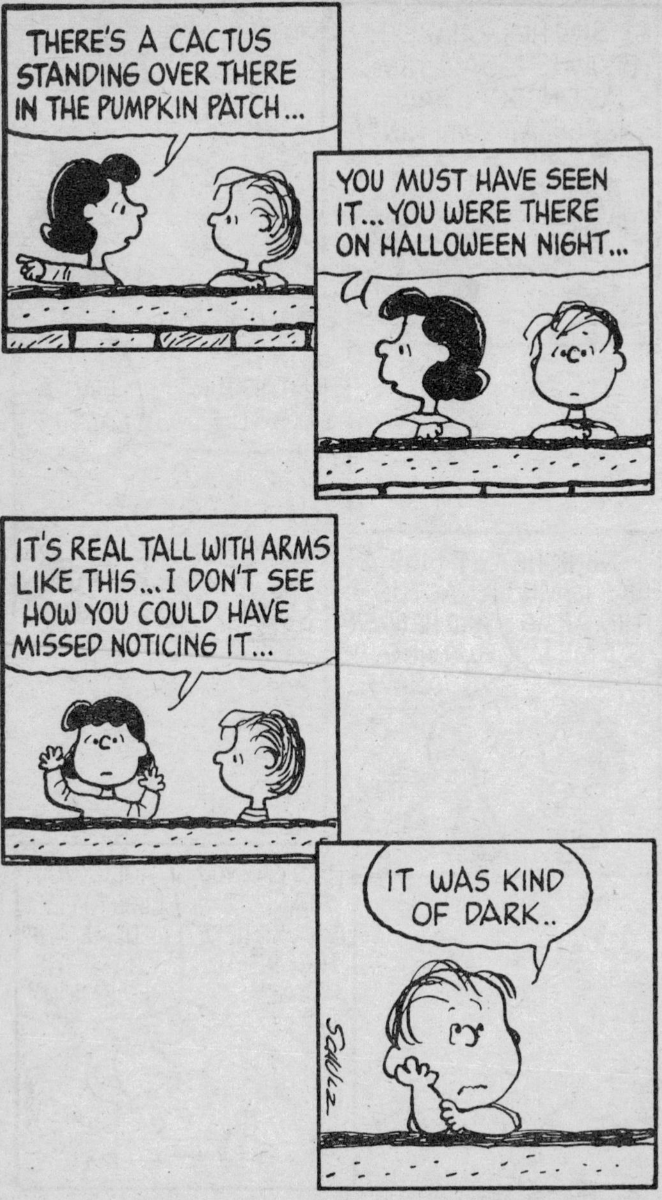
THERE'S A CACTUS STANDING OVER THERE IN THE PUMPKIN PATCH...
YOU MUST HAVE SEEN IT...YOU WERE THERE ON HALLOWEEN NIGHT...
IT'S REAL TALL WITH ARMS LIKE THIS...I DON'T SEE HOW YOU COULD HAVE MISSED NOTICING IT...
IT WAS KIND OF DARK..
SCHULZ

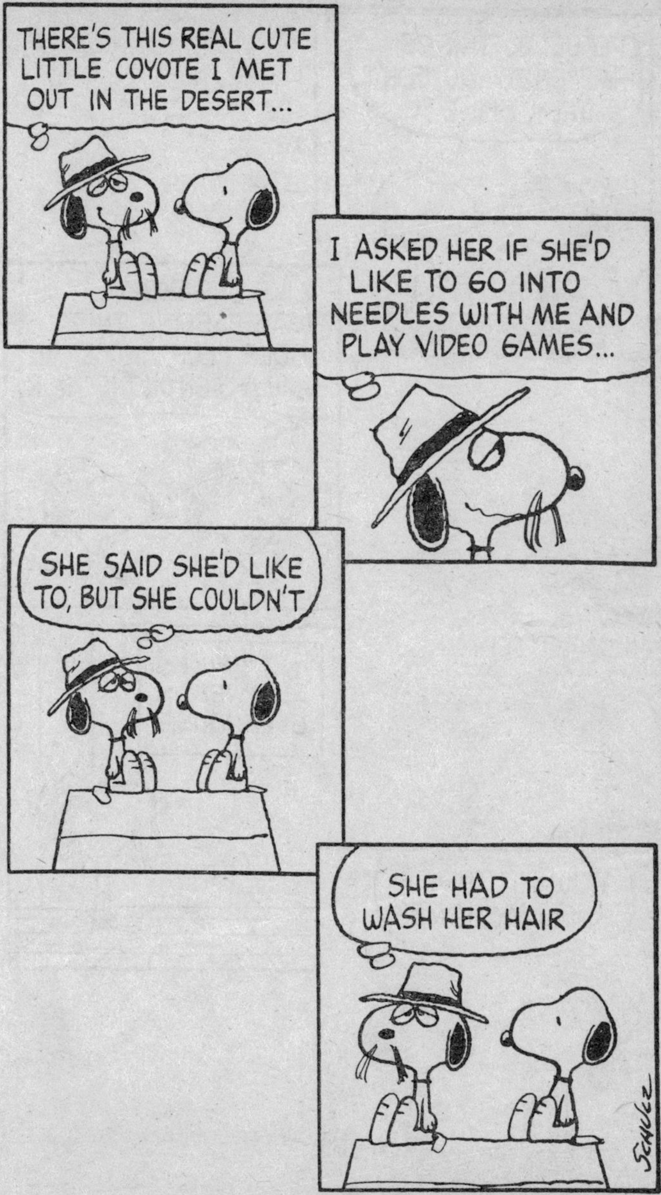
THERE'S THIS REAL CUTE LITTLE COYOTE I MET OUT IN THE DESERT...
I ASKED HER IF SHE'D LIKE TO GO INTO NEEDLES WITH ME AND PLAY VIDEO GAMES...
SHE SAID SHE'D LIKE TO, BUT SHE COULDN'T
SHE HAD TO WASH HER HAIR
SCHULZ

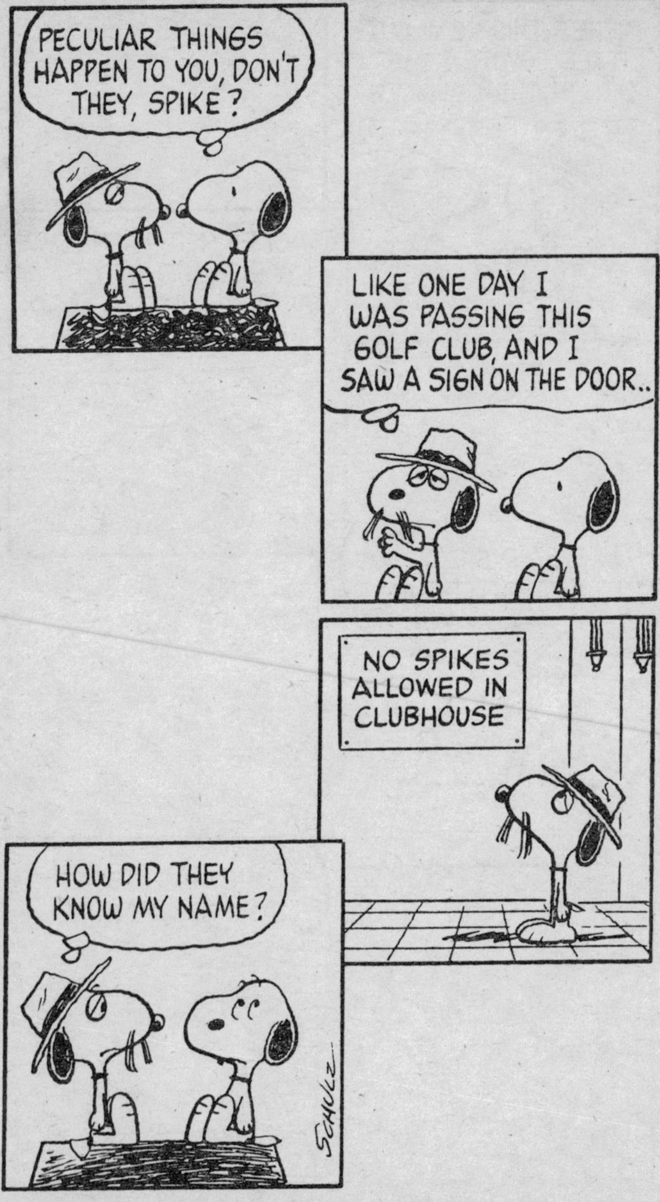
PECULIAR THINGS HAPPEN TO YOU, DON'T THEY, SPIKE?
LIKE ONE DAY I WAS PASSING THIS GOLF CLUB, AND I SAW A SIGN ON THE DOOR..
NO SPIKES ALLOWED IN CLUBHOUSE
HOW DID THEY KNOW MY NAME?
SCHULZ

BEFORE YOU LEAVE, SPIKE, TELL ME ONE MORE STORY...

I WAS IN A FOX HUNT ONCE NEAR MARSHALL, VIRGINIA WITH ABOUT FIFTY OTHER BEAGLES...

I GOT LOST, BUT THE FOX FOUND ME AND TOOK ME BACK...IT WAS VERY EMBARRASSING

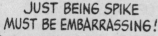

JUST BEING SPIKE MUST BE EMBARRASSING!

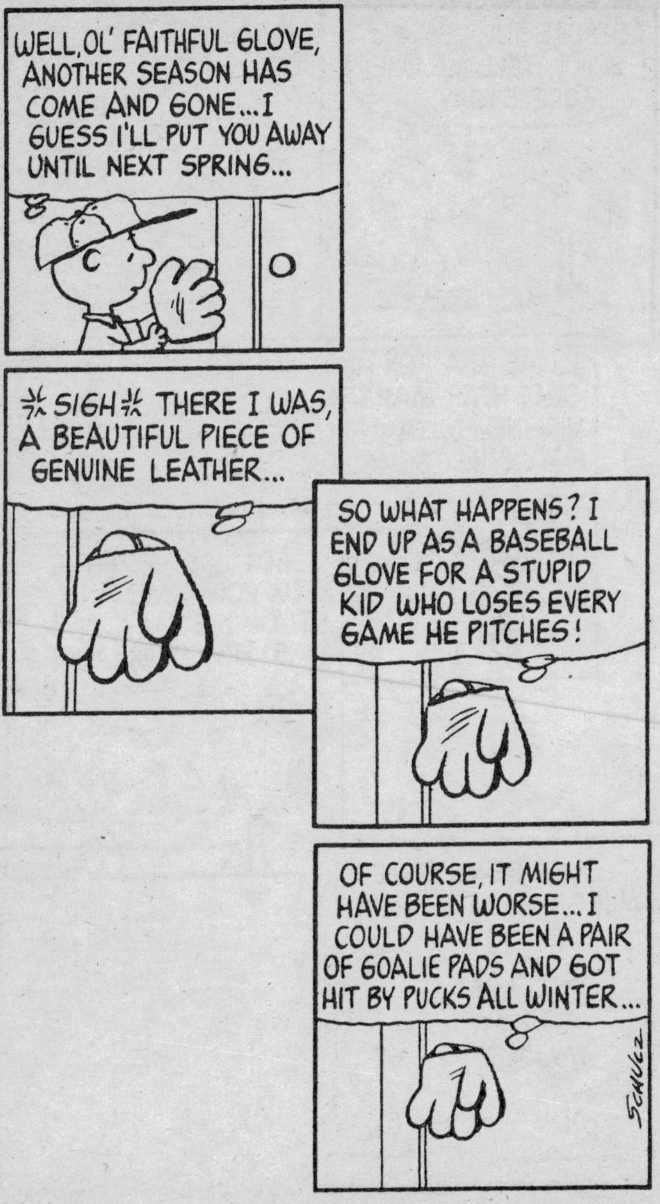

WELL, OL' FAITHFUL GLOVE, ANOTHER SEASON HAS COME AND GONE...I GUESS I'LL PUT YOU AWAY UNTIL NEXT SPRING...
SIGH THERE I WAS, A BEAUTIFUL PIECE OF GENUINE LEATHER...
SO WHAT HAPPENS? I END UP AS A BASEBALL GLOVE FOR A STUPID KID WHO LOSES EVERY GAME HE PITCHES!
OF COURSE, IT MIGHT HAVE BEEN WORSE...I COULD HAVE BEEN A PAIR OF GOALIE PADS AND GOT HIT BY PUCKS ALL WINTER...
SCHULZ

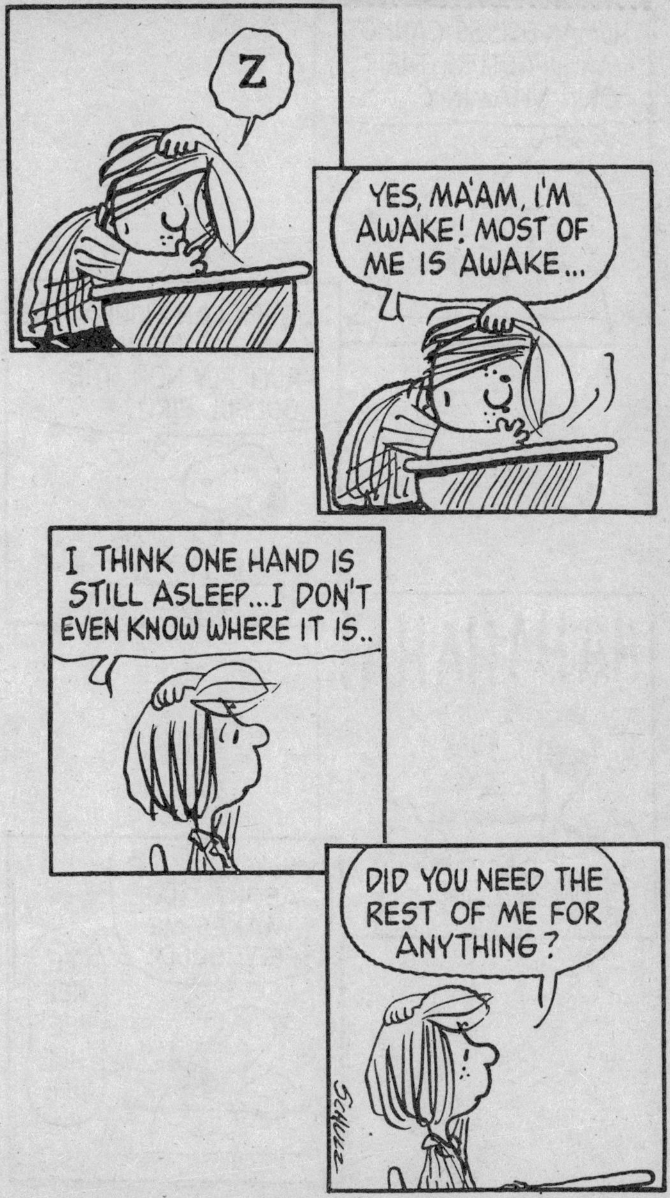

Z
YES, MA'AM, I'M AWAKE! MOST OF ME IS AWAKE...
I THINK ONE HAND IS STILL ASLEEP...I DON'T EVEN KNOW WHERE IT IS..
DID YOU NEED THE REST OF ME FOR ANYTHING?
SCHULZ

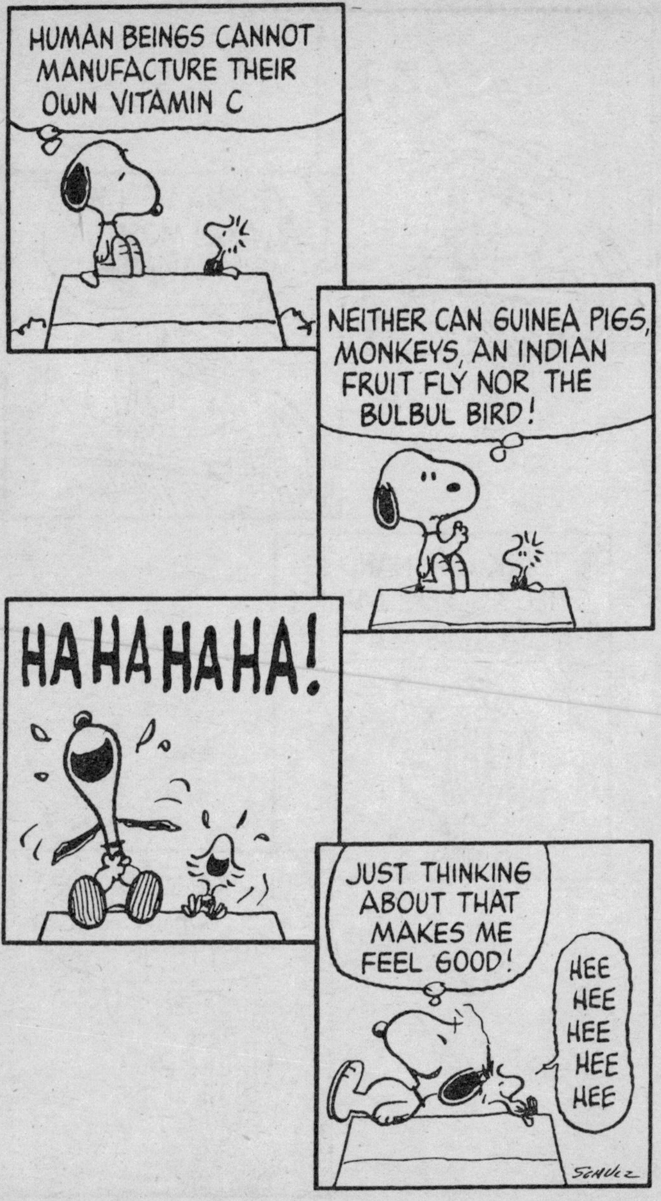
HUMAN BEINGS CANNOT MANUFACTURE THEIR OWN VITAMIN C
NEITHER CAN GUINEA PIGS, MONKEYS, AN INDIAN FRUIT FLY NOR THE BULBUL BIRD!
HAHAHAHAHA!
JUST THINKING ABOUT THAT MAKES ME FEEL GOOD!
HEE HEE HEE HEE HEE
SCHULZ

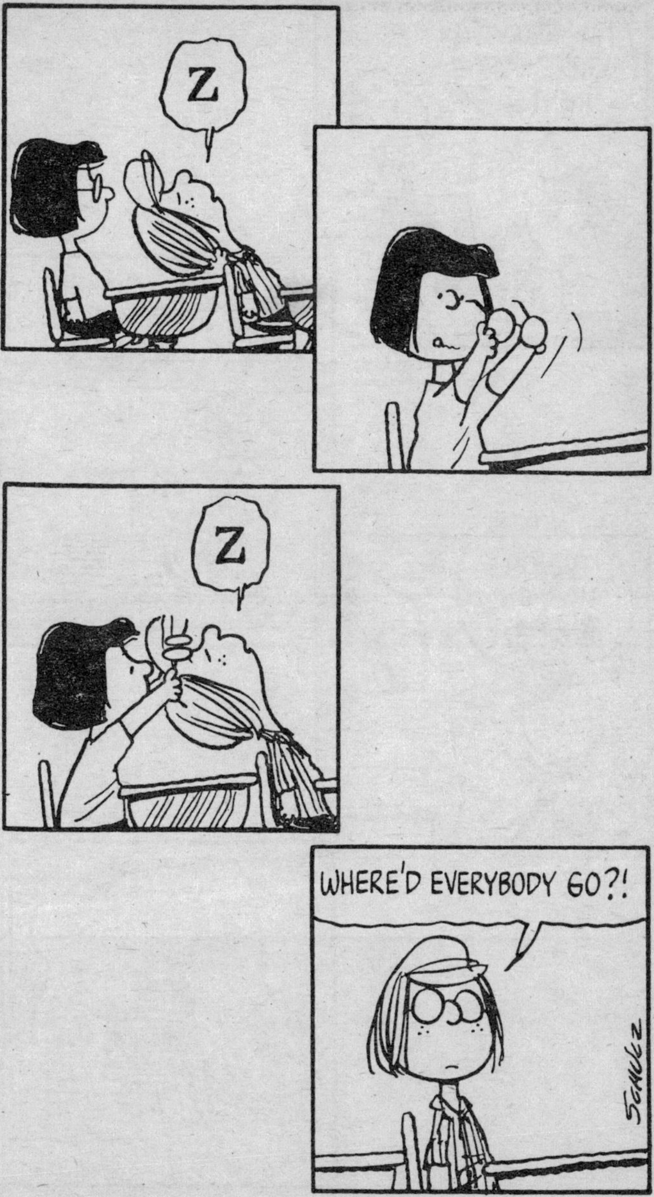
Z
Z
WHERE'D EVERYBODY GO?!
SCHULZ

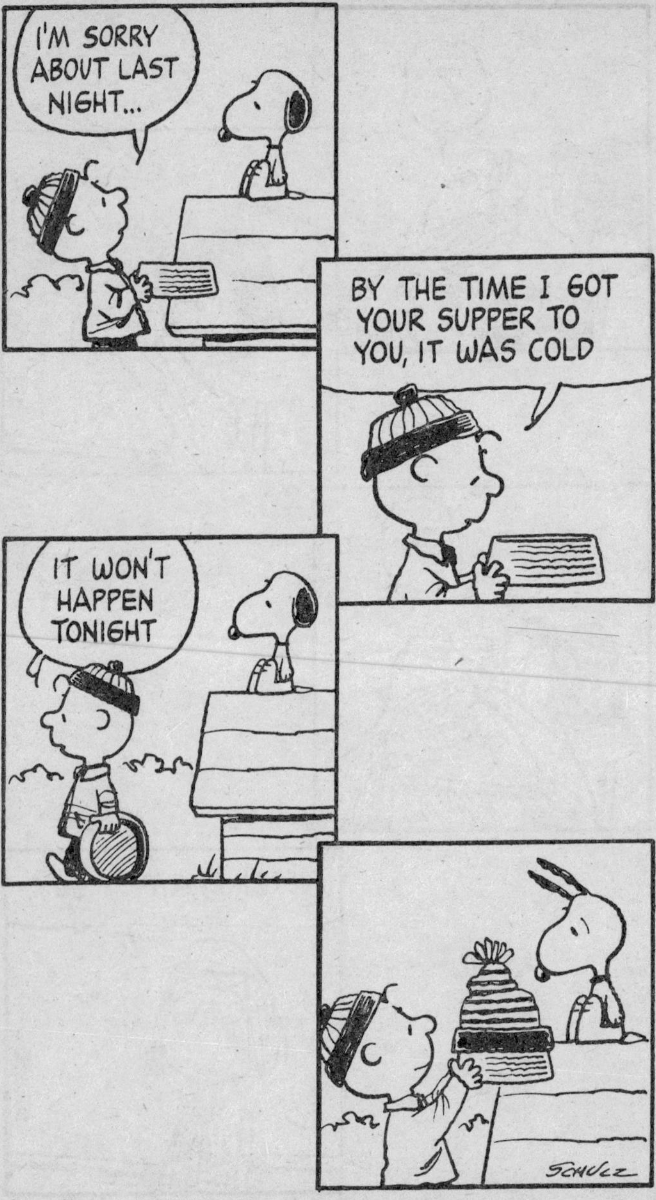
I'M SORRY ABOUT LAST NIGHT...
BY THE TIME I GOT YOUR SUPPER TO YOU, IT WAS COLD
IT WON'T HAPPEN TONIGHT
SCHULZ

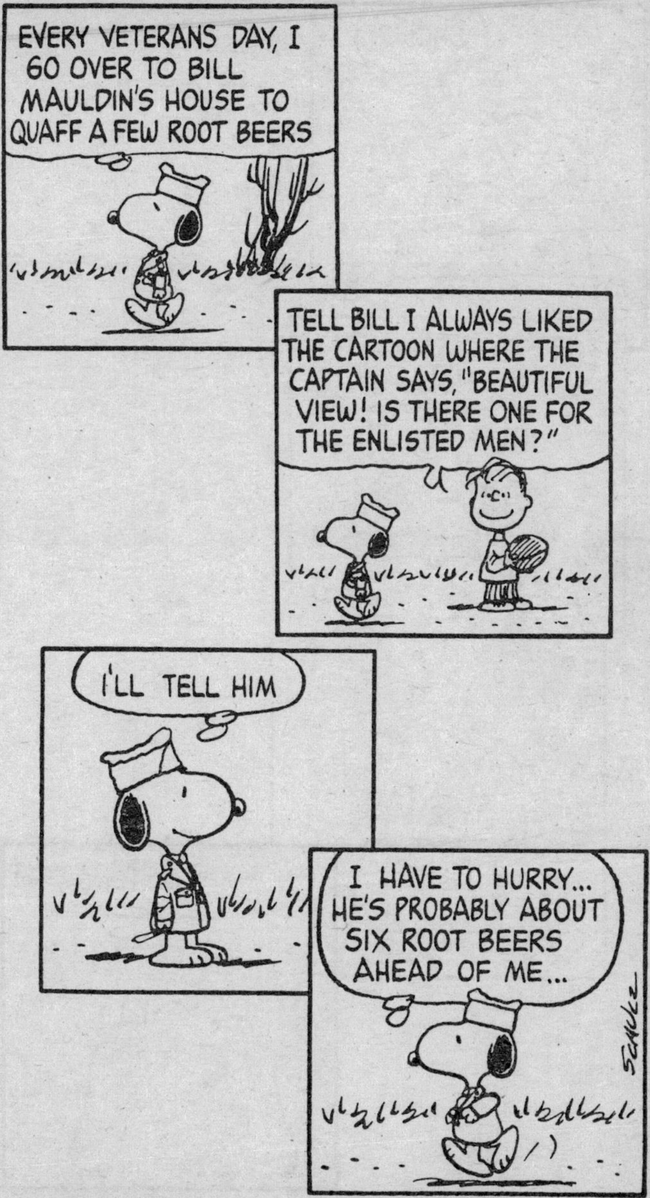

EVERY VETERANS DAY, I GO OVER TO BILL MAULDIN'S HOUSE TO QUAFF A FEW ROOT BEERS
TELL BILL I ALWAYS LIKED THE CARTOON WHERE THE CAPTAIN SAYS, "BEAUTIFUL VIEW! IS THERE ONE FOR THE ENLISTED MEN?"
I'LL TELL HIM
I HAVE TO HURRY... HE'S PROBABLY ABOUT SIX ROOT BEERS AHEAD OF ME...
SCHULZ

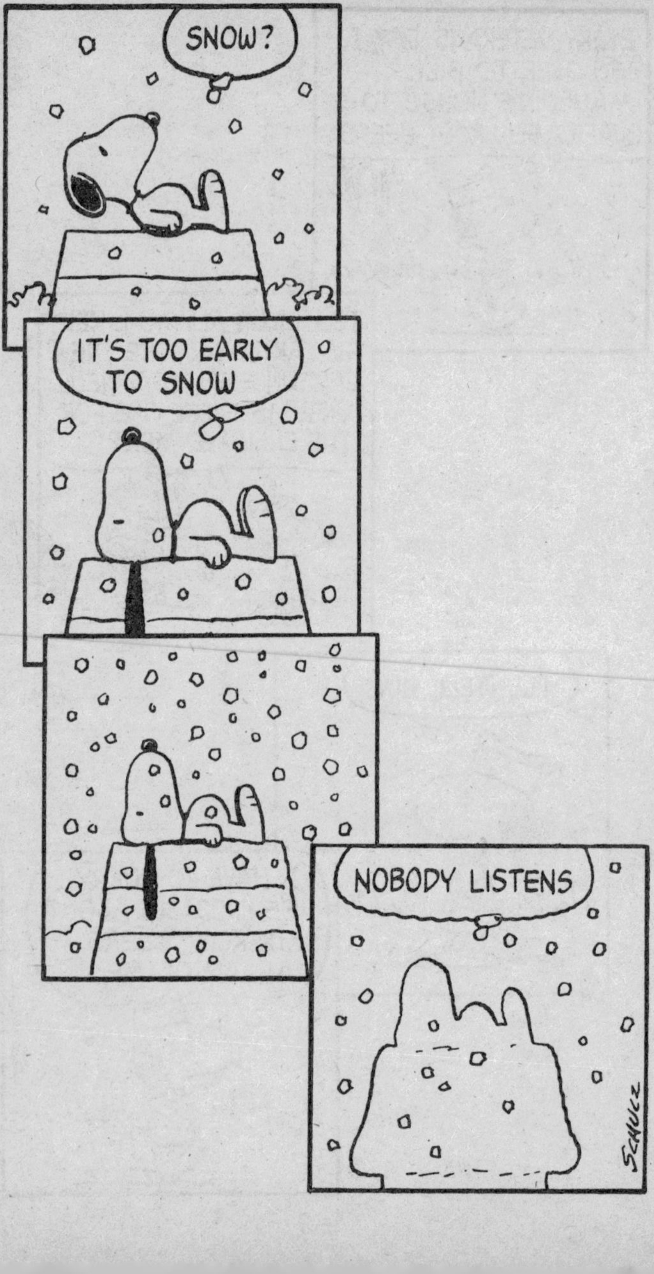
SNOW?
IT'S TOO EARLY TO SNOW
NOBODY LISTENS
SCHULZ

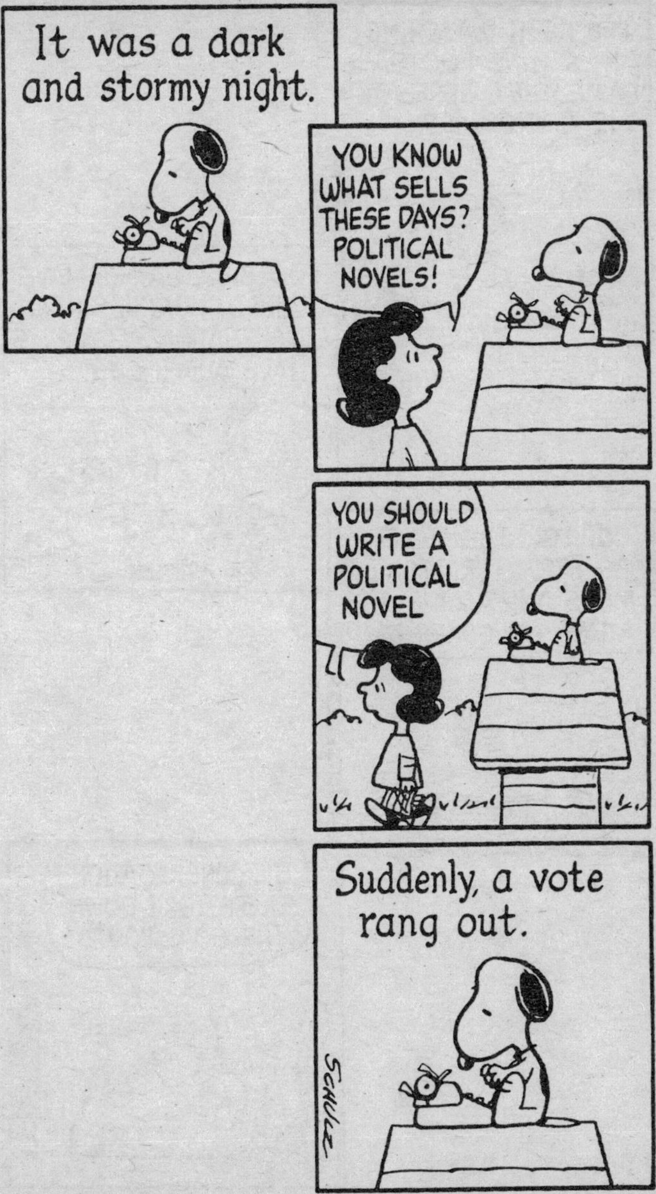
It was a dark and stormy night.
YOU KNOW WHAT SELLS THESE DAYS? POLITICAL NOVELS!
YOU SHOULD WRITE A POLITICAL NOVEL
Suddenly, a vote rang out.
SCHULZ

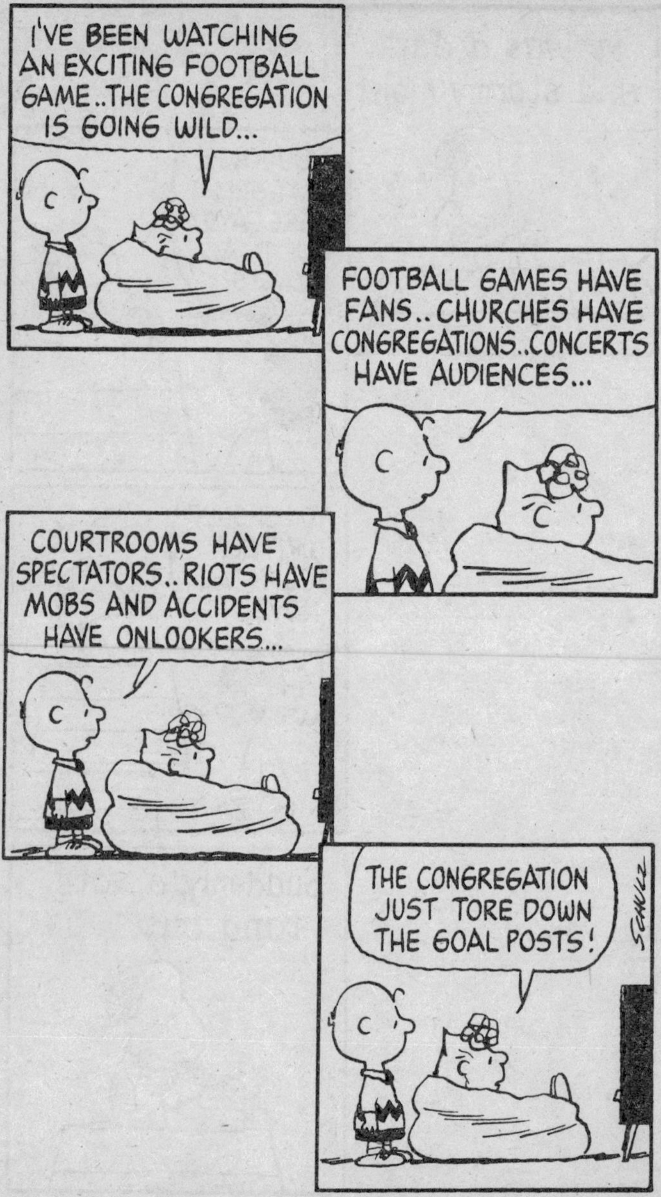
I'VE BEEN WATCHING AN EXCITING FOOTBALL GAME..THE CONGREGATION IS GOING WILD...
FOOTBALL GAMES HAVE FANS..CHURCHES HAVE CONGREGATIONS..CONCERTS HAVE AUDIENCES...
COURTROOMS HAVE SPECTATORS..RIOTS HAVE MOBS AND ACCIDENTS HAVE ONLOOKERS...
THE CONGREGATION JUST TORE DOWN THE GOAL POSTS!
SCHULZ

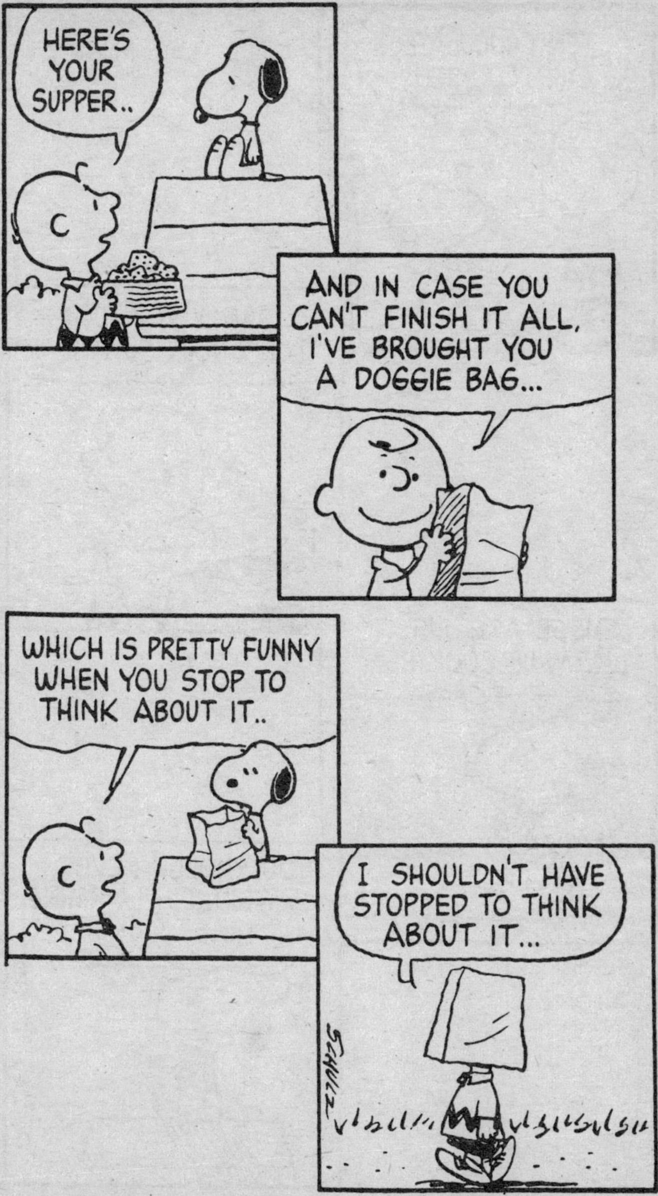
HERE'S YOUR SUPPER..
AND IN CASE YOU CAN'T FINISH IT ALL, I'VE BROUGHT YOU A DOGGIE BAG...
WHICH IS PRETTY FUNNY WHEN YOU STOP TO THINK ABOUT IT..
I SHOULDN'T HAVE STOPPED TO THINK ABOUT IT...
SCHULZ

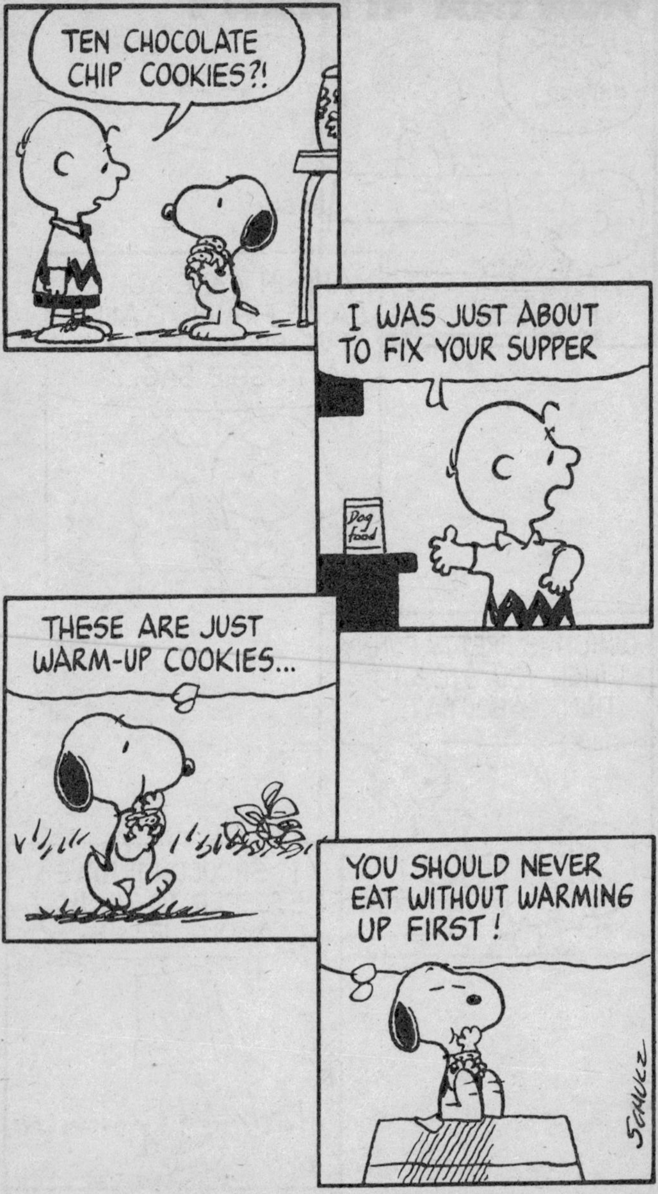
TEN CHOCOLATE CHIP COOKIES?!
I WAS JUST ABOUT TO FIX YOUR SUPPER
Dog food
THESE ARE JUST WARM-UP COOKIES...
YOU SHOULD NEVER EAT WITHOUT WARMING UP FIRST!
SCHULZ

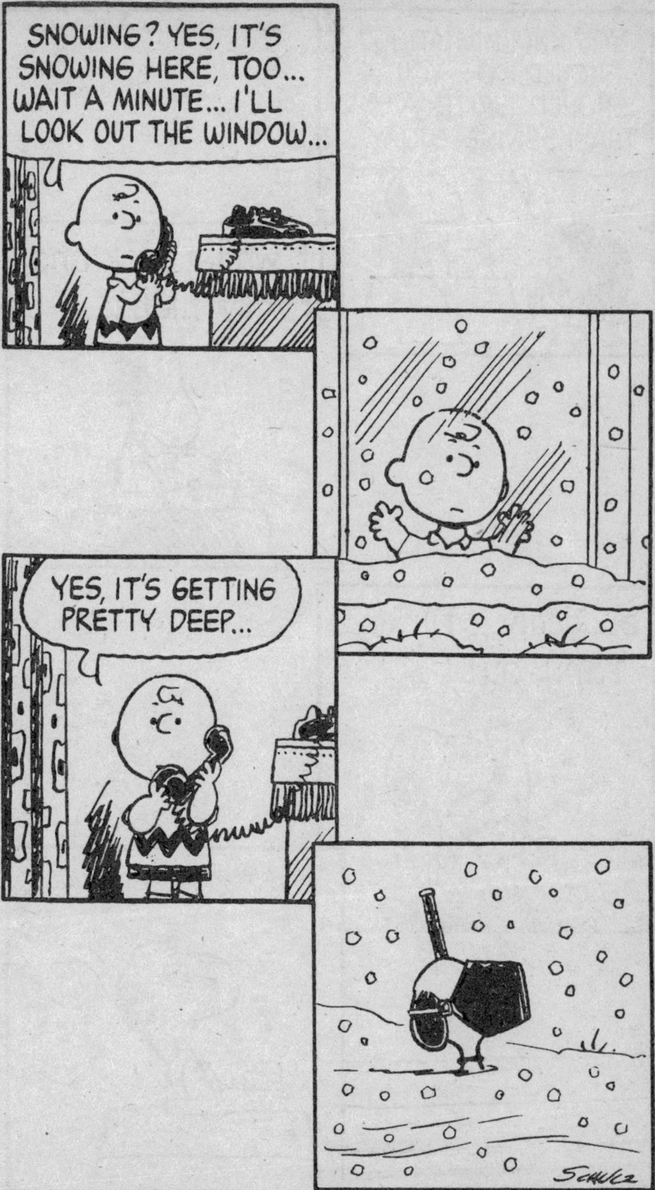
SNOWING? YES, IT'S SNOWING HERE, TOO... WAIT A MINUTE... I'LL LOOK OUT THE WINDOW...
YES, IT'S GETTING PRETTY DEEP...
SCHULZ

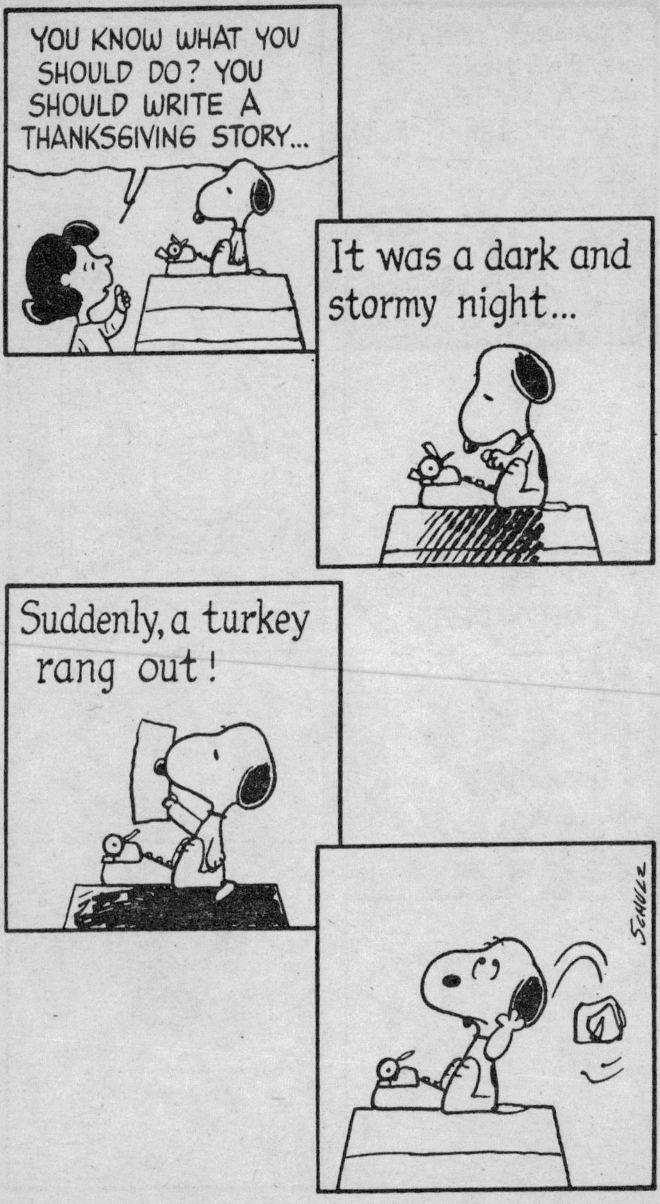
YOU KNOW WHAT YOU SHOULD DO? YOU SHOULD WRITE A THANKSGIVING STORY...
It was a dark and stormy night...
Suddenly, a turkey rang out!
SCHULZ

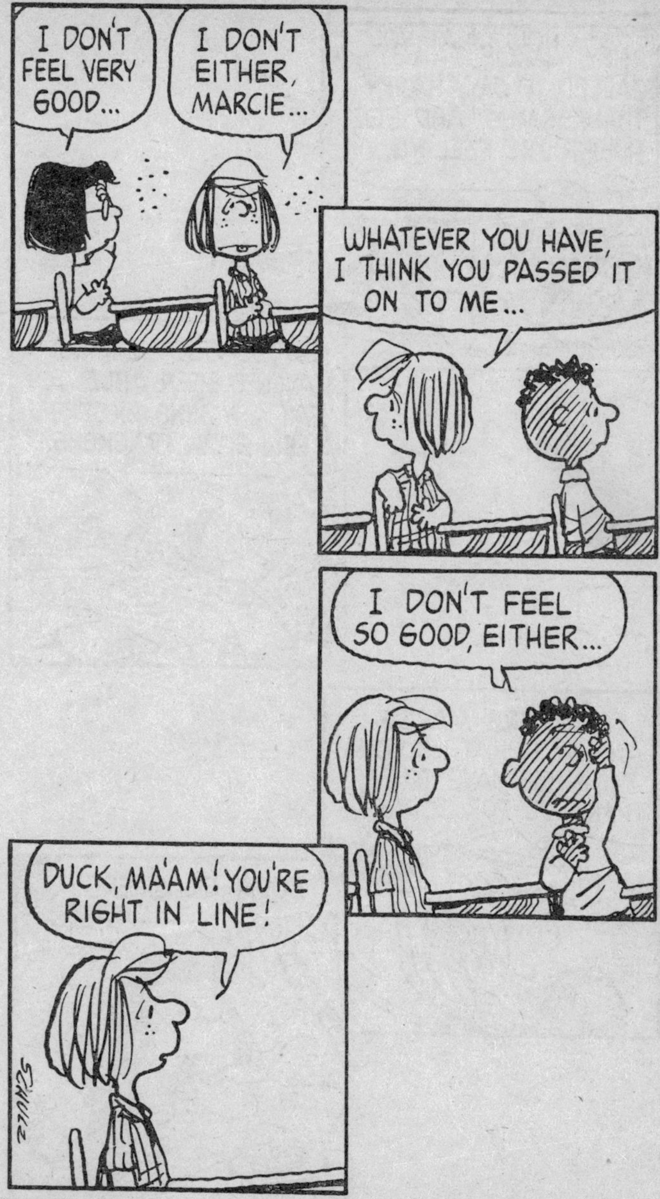

I DON'T FEEL VERY GOOD...
I DON'T EITHER, MARCIE...
WHATEVER YOU HAVE, I THINK YOU PASSED IT ON TO ME...
I DON'T FEEL SO GOOD, EITHER...
DUCK, MA'AM! YOU'RE RIGHT IN LINE!
SCHULZ

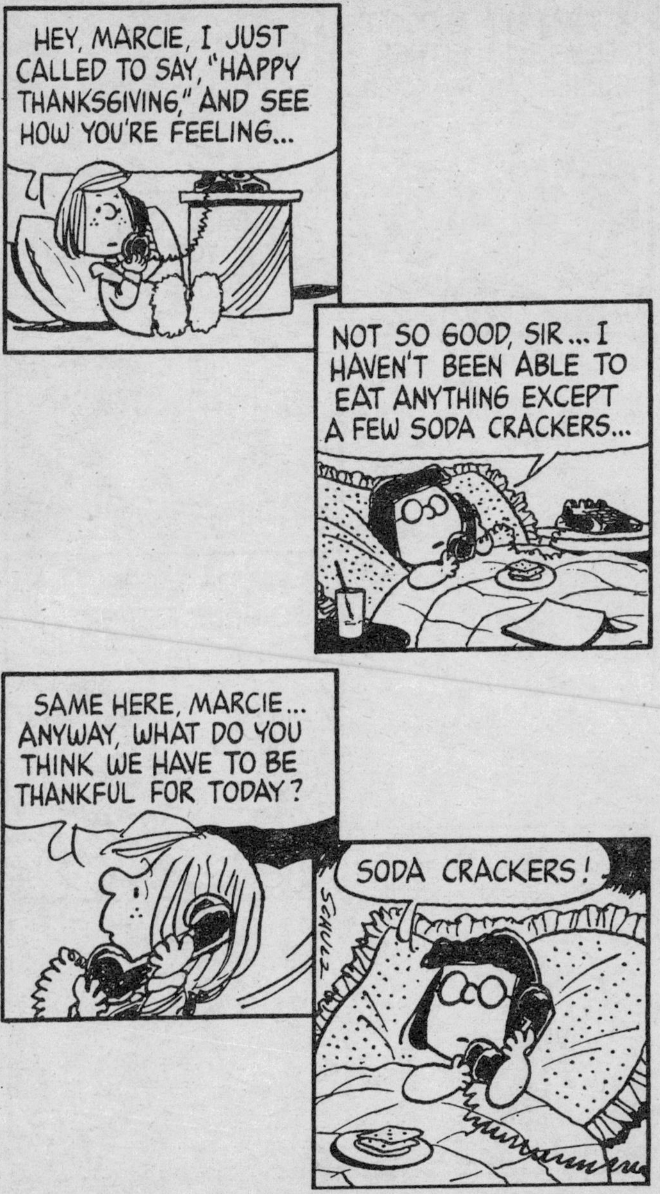
HEY, MARCIE, I JUST CALLED TO SAY, "HAPPY THANKSGIVING," AND SEE HOW YOU'RE FEELING...
NOT SO GOOD, SIR... I HAVEN'T BEEN ABLE TO EAT ANYTHING EXCEPT A FEW SODA CRACKERS...
SAME HERE, MARCIE... ANYWAY, WHAT DO YOU THINK WE HAVE TO BE THANKFUL FOR TODAY?
SODA CRACKERS!
SCHULZ

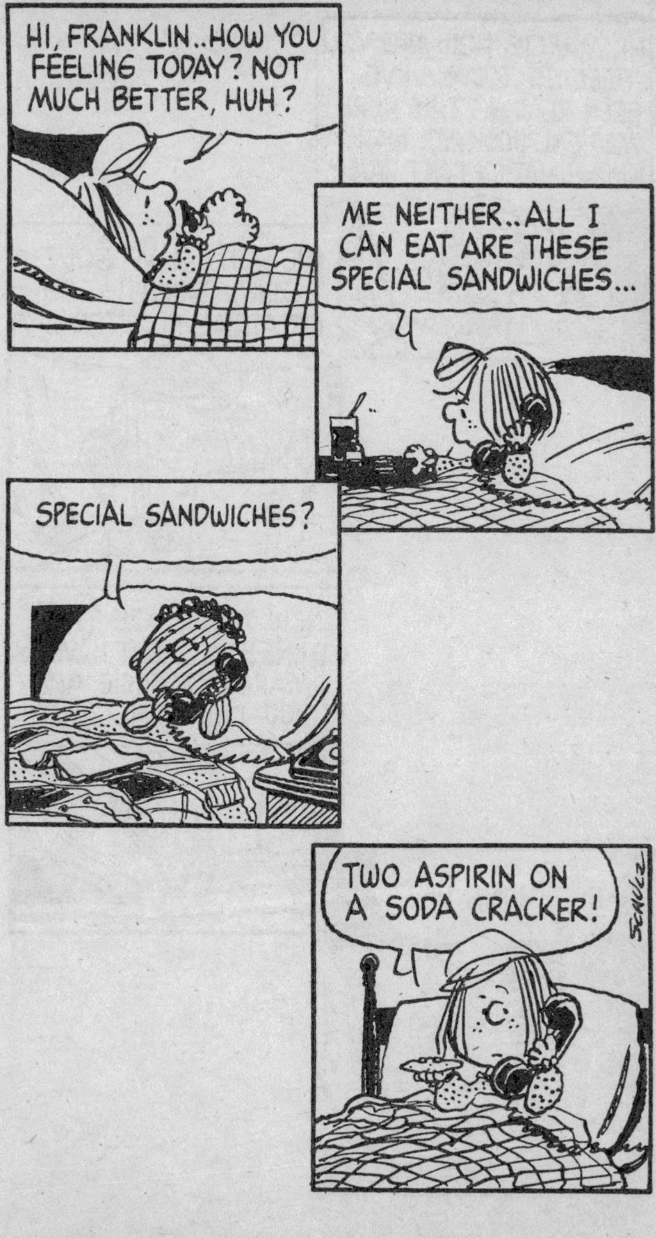
HI, FRANKLIN..HOW YOU FEELING TODAY? NOT MUCH BETTER, HUH?
ME NEITHER..ALL I CAN EAT ARE THESE SPECIAL SANDWICHES...
SPECIAL SANDWICHES?
TWO ASPIRIN ON A SODA CRACKER!
SCHULZ

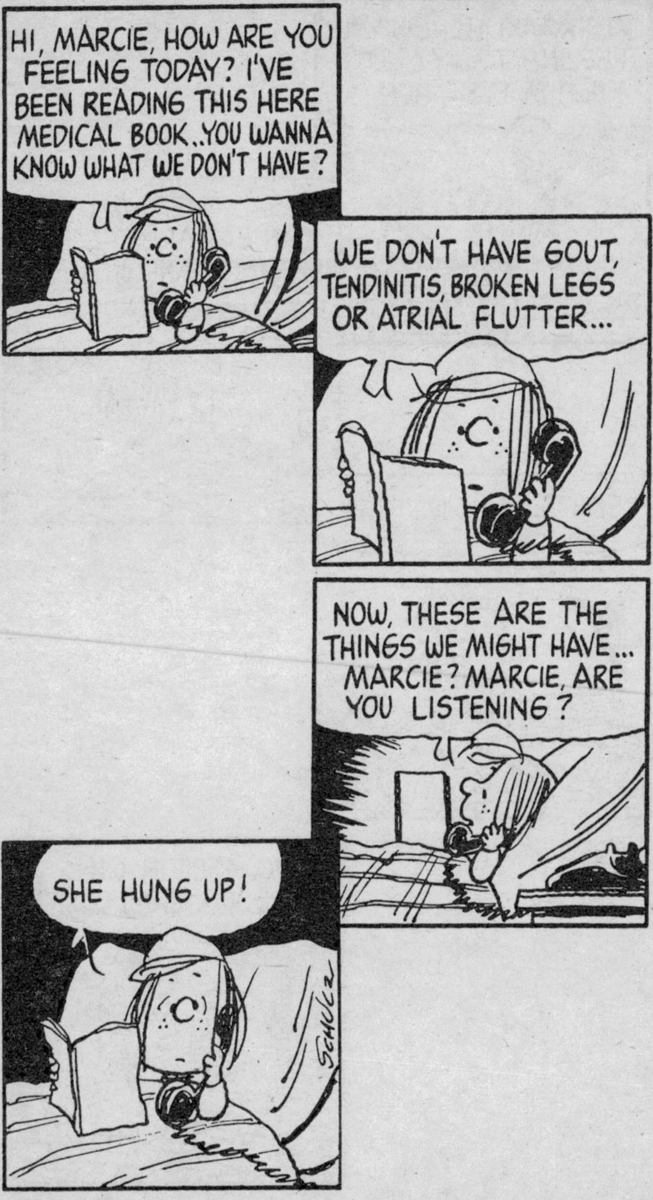
HI, MARCIE, HOW ARE YOU FEELING TODAY? I'VE BEEN READING THIS HERE MEDICAL BOOK..YOU WANNA KNOW WHAT WE DON'T HAVE?
WE DON'T HAVE GOUT, TENDINITIS, BROKEN LEGS OR ATRIAL FLUTTER...
NOW, THESE ARE THE THINGS WE MIGHT HAVE... MARCIE? MARCIE, ARE YOU LISTENING?
SHE HUNG UP!
SCHULZ

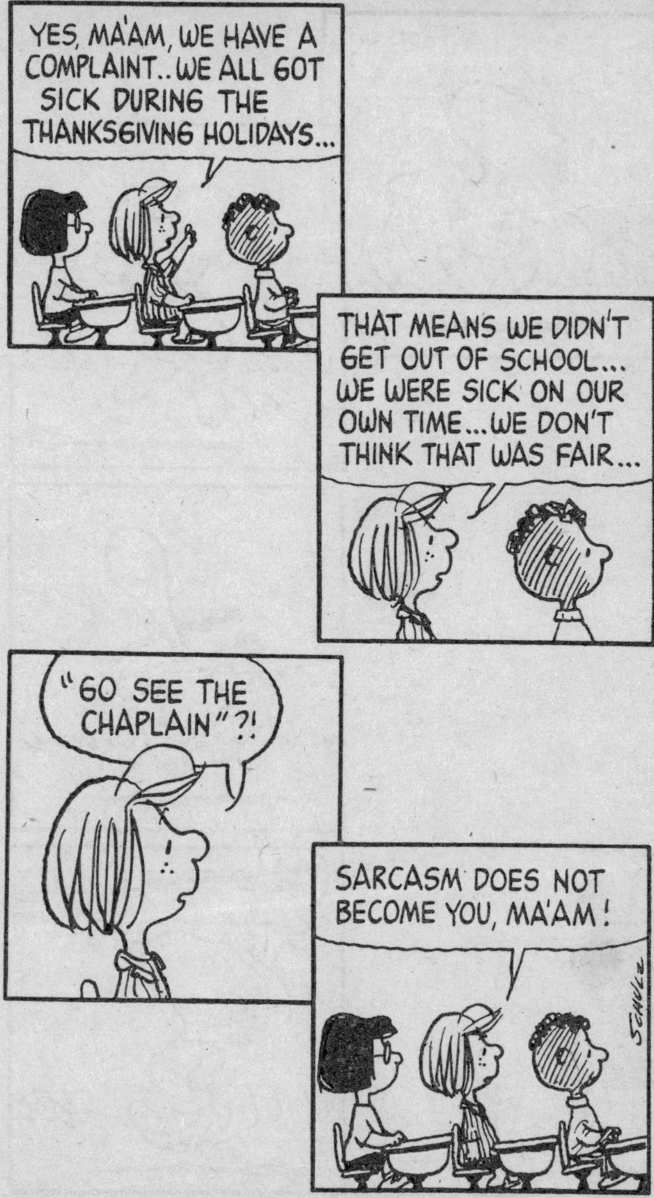
YES, MA'AM, WE HAVE A COMPLAINT.. WE ALL GOT SICK DURING THE THANKSGIVING HOLIDAYS...
THAT MEANS WE DIDN'T GET OUT OF SCHOOL... WE WERE SICK ON OUR OWN TIME... WE DON'T THINK THAT WAS FAIR...
"GO SEE THE CHAPLAIN"?!
SARCASM DOES NOT BECOME YOU, MA'AM!
SCHULZ

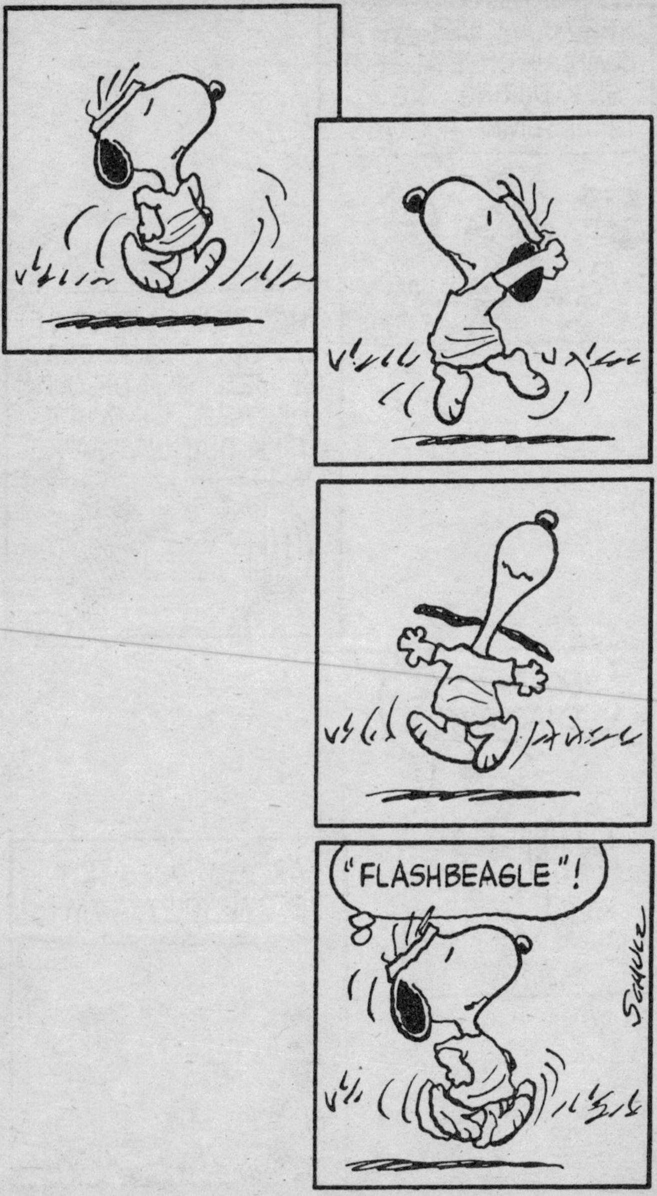
"FLASHBEAGLE"!
SCHULZ

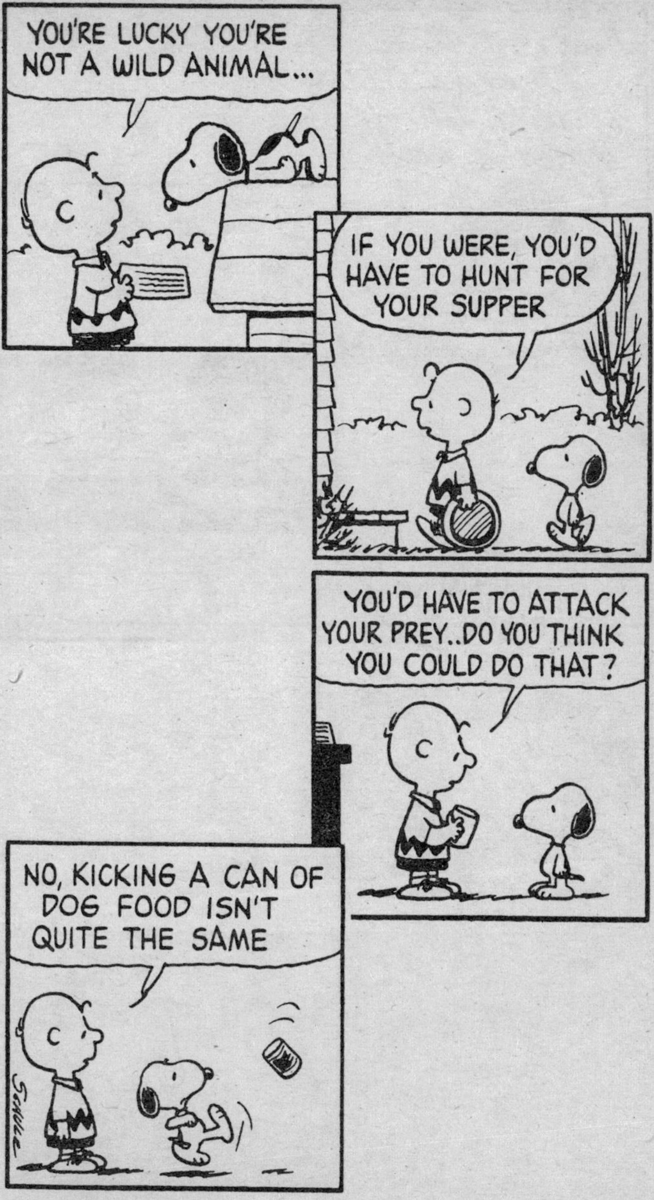
YOU'RE LUCKY YOU'RE NOT A WILD ANIMAL...
IF YOU WERE, YOU'D HAVE TO HUNT FOR YOUR SUPPER
YOU'D HAVE TO ATTACK YOUR PREY..DO YOU THINK YOU COULD DO THAT?
NO, KICKING A CAN OF DOG FOOD ISN'T QUITE THE SAME

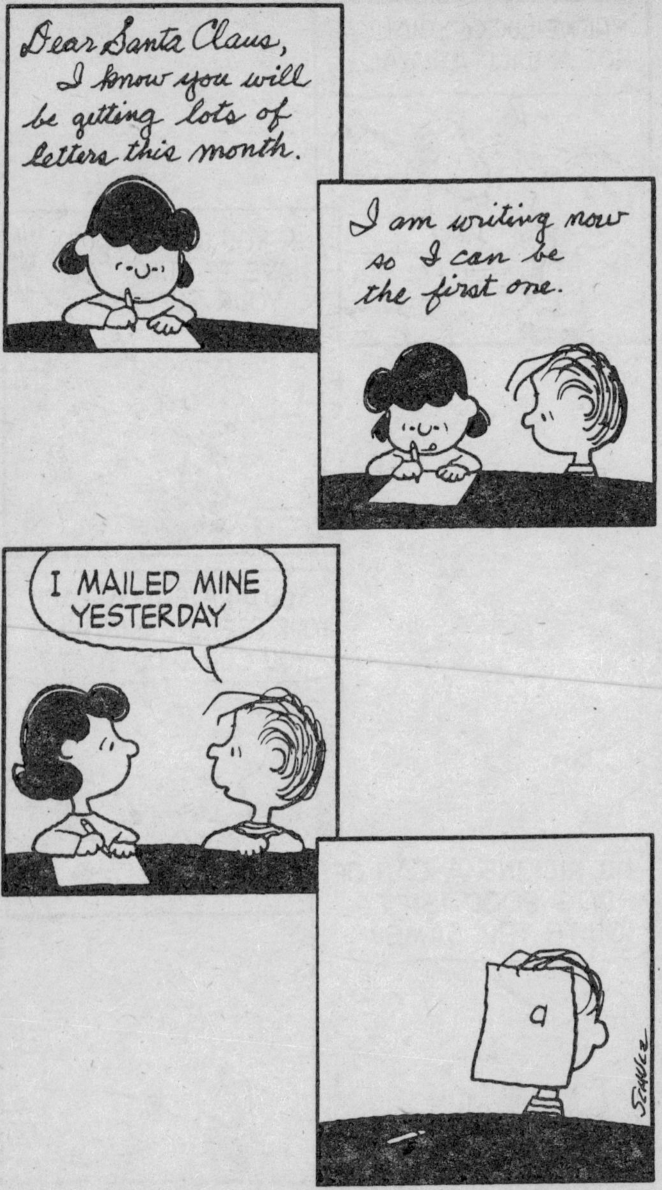

Dear Santa Claus,
I know you will be getting lots of letters this month.
I am writing now so I can be the first one.
I MAILED MINE YESTERDAY
SCHULZ

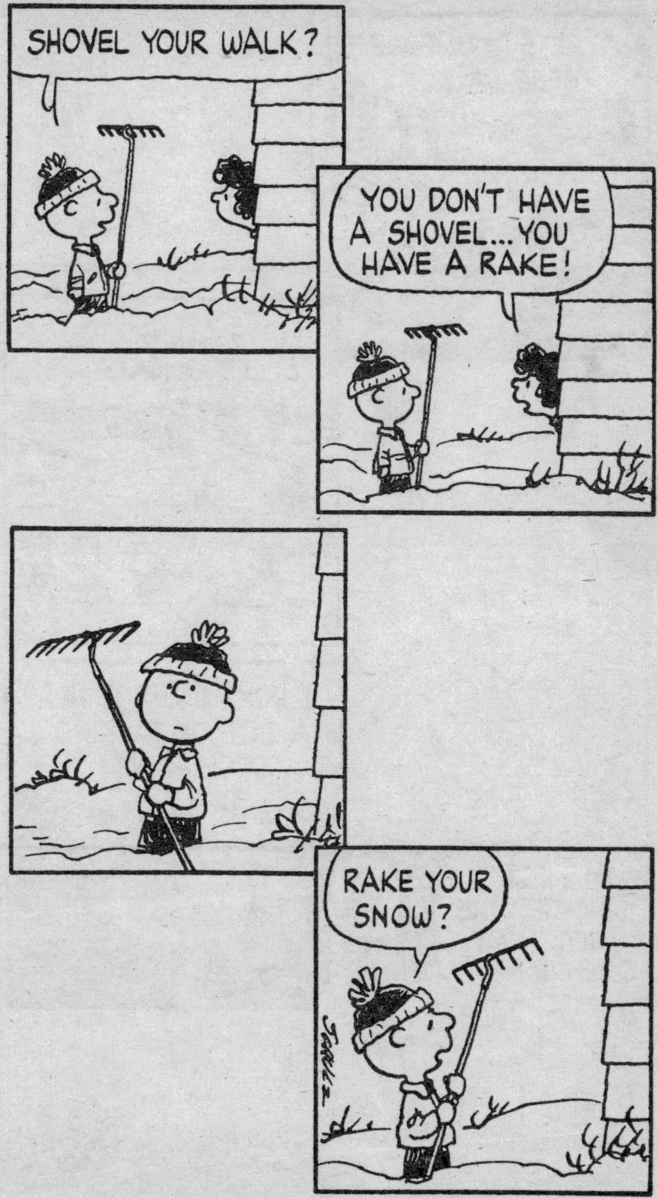
SHOVEL YOUR WALK?
YOU DON'T HAVE A SHOVEL... YOU HAVE A RAKE!
RAKE YOUR SNOW?

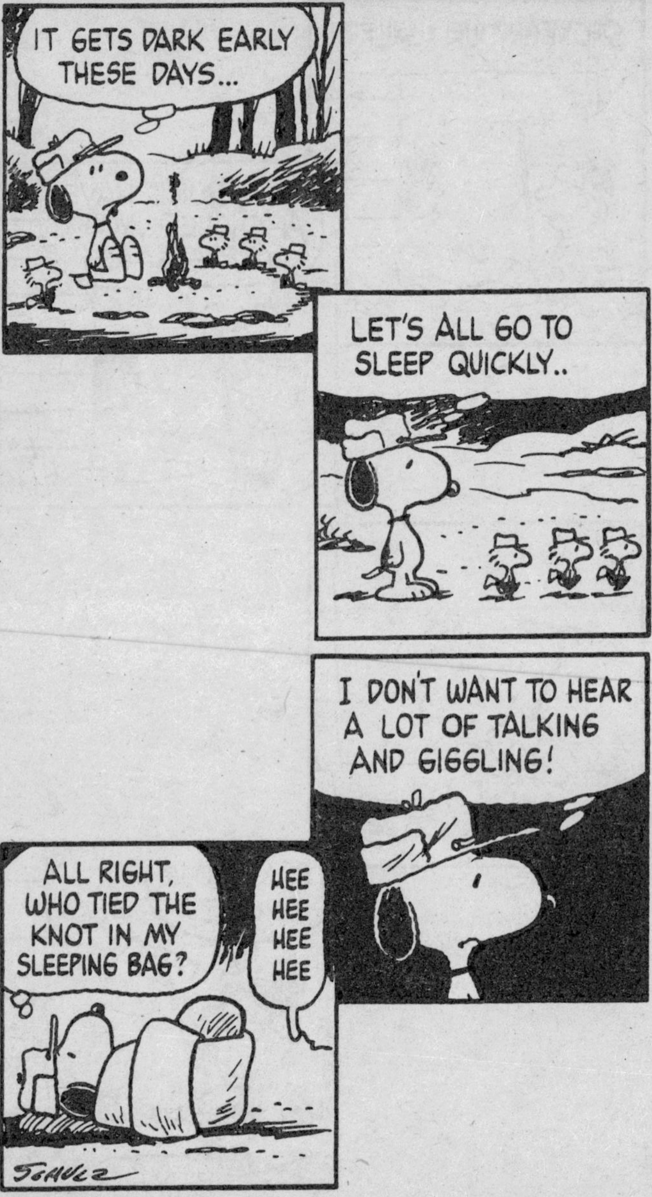
IT GETS DARK EARLY THESE DAYS...
LET'S ALL GO TO SLEEP QUICKLY..
I DON'T WANT TO HEAR A LOT OF TALKING AND GIGGLING!
ALL RIGHT, WHO TIED THE KNOT IN MY SLEEPING BAG?
HEE HEE HEE HEE
SCHULZ

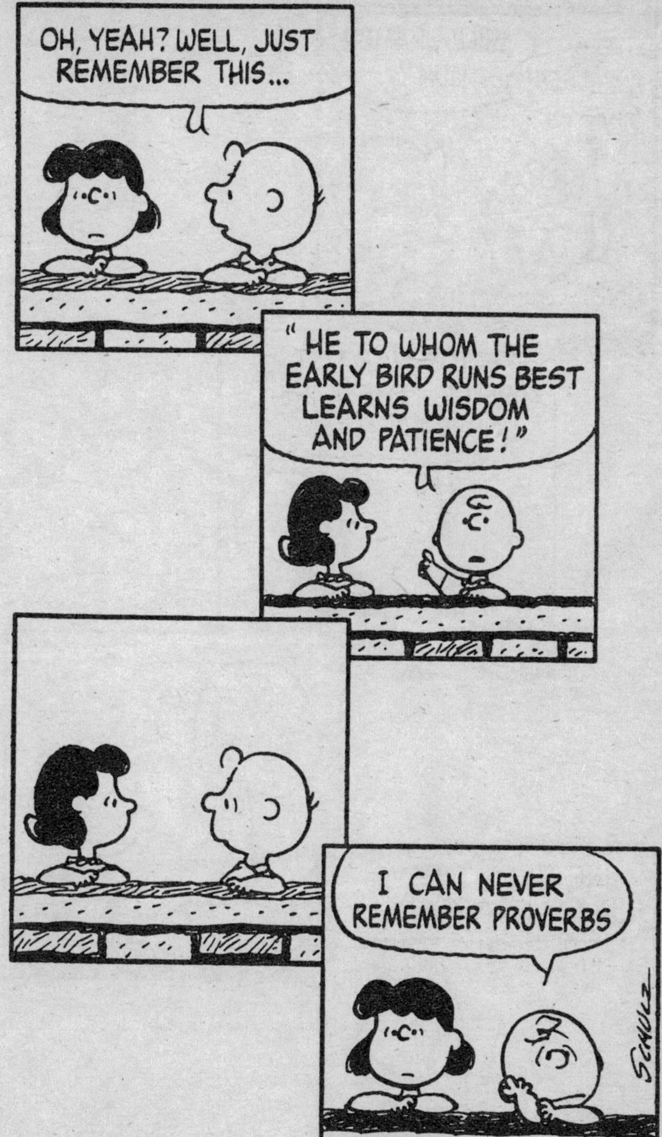
OH, YEAH? WELL, JUST REMEMBER THIS...
"HE TO WHOM THE EARLY BIRD RUNS BEST LEARNS WISDOM AND PATIENCE!"
I CAN NEVER REMEMBER PROVERBS
SCHULZ

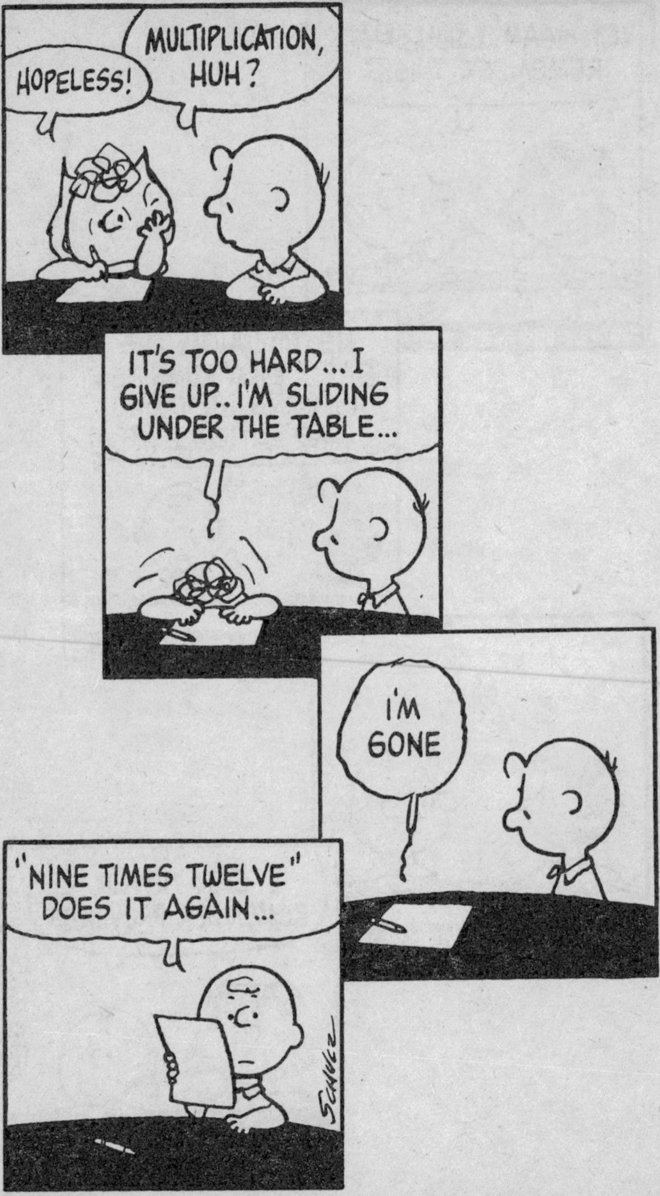
MULTIPLICATION, HUH?
HOPELESS!
IT'S TOO HARD... I GIVE UP.. I'M SLIDING UNDER THE TABLE...
I'M GONE
"NINE TIMES TWELVE" DOES IT AGAIN...
SCHULZ

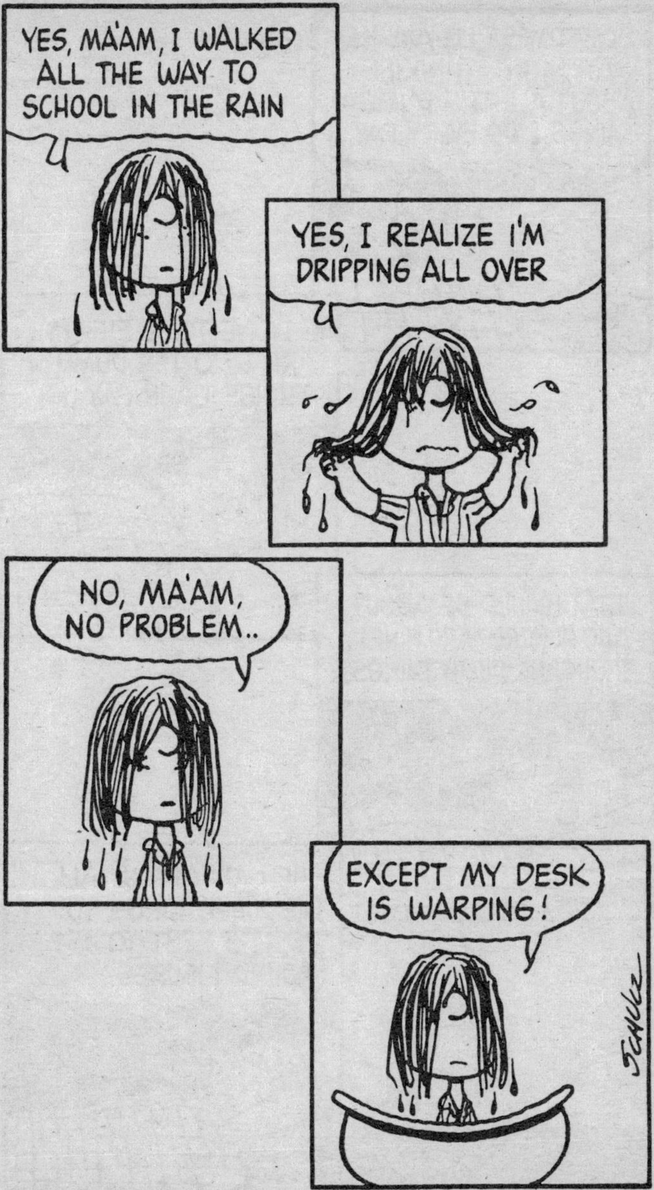
YES, MA'AM, I WALKED ALL THE WAY TO SCHOOL IN THE RAIN
YES, I REALIZE I'M DRIPPING ALL OVER
NO, MA'AM, NO PROBLEM..
EXCEPT MY DESK IS WARPING!

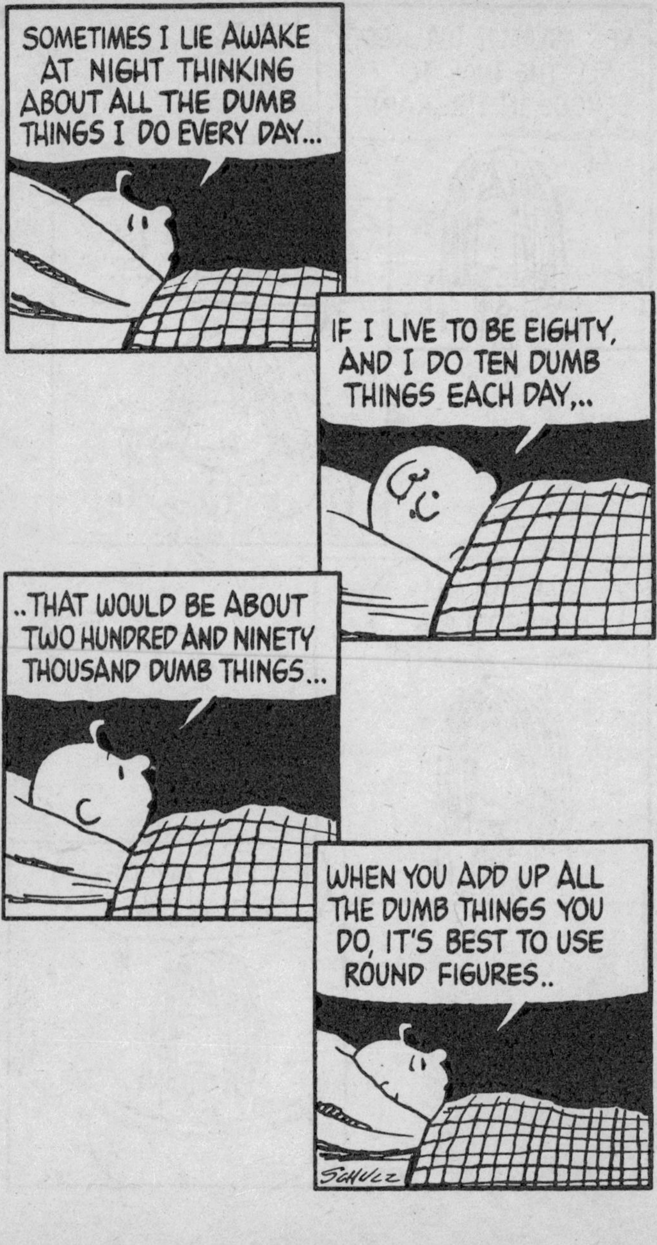
SOMETIMES I LIE AWAKE AT NIGHT THINKING ABOUT ALL THE DUMB THINGS I DO EVERY DAY...
IF I LIVE TO BE EIGHTY, AND I DO TEN DUMB THINGS EACH DAY,...
..THAT WOULD BE ABOUT TWO HUNDRED AND NINETY THOUSAND DUMB THINGS...
WHEN YOU ADD UP ALL THE DUMB THINGS YOU DO, IT'S BEST TO USE ROUND FIGURES..
SCHULZ

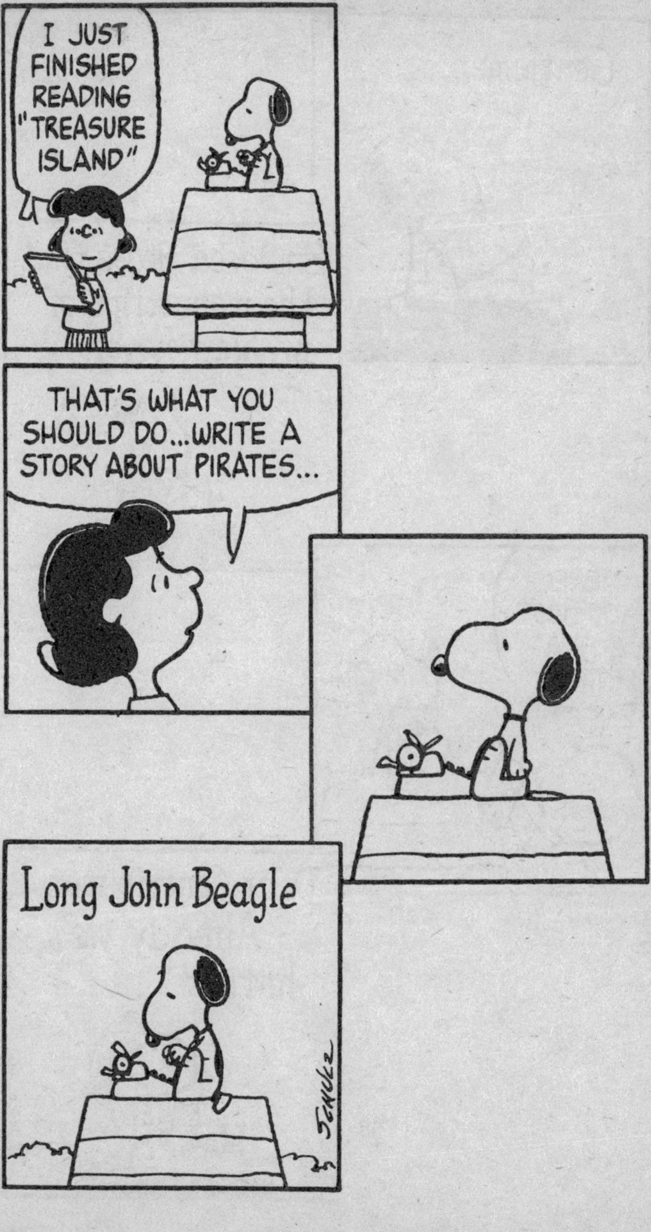
I JUST FINISHED READING "TREASURE ISLAND"
THAT'S WHAT YOU SHOULD DO...WRITE A STORY ABOUT PIRATES...
Long John Beagle
SCHULZ

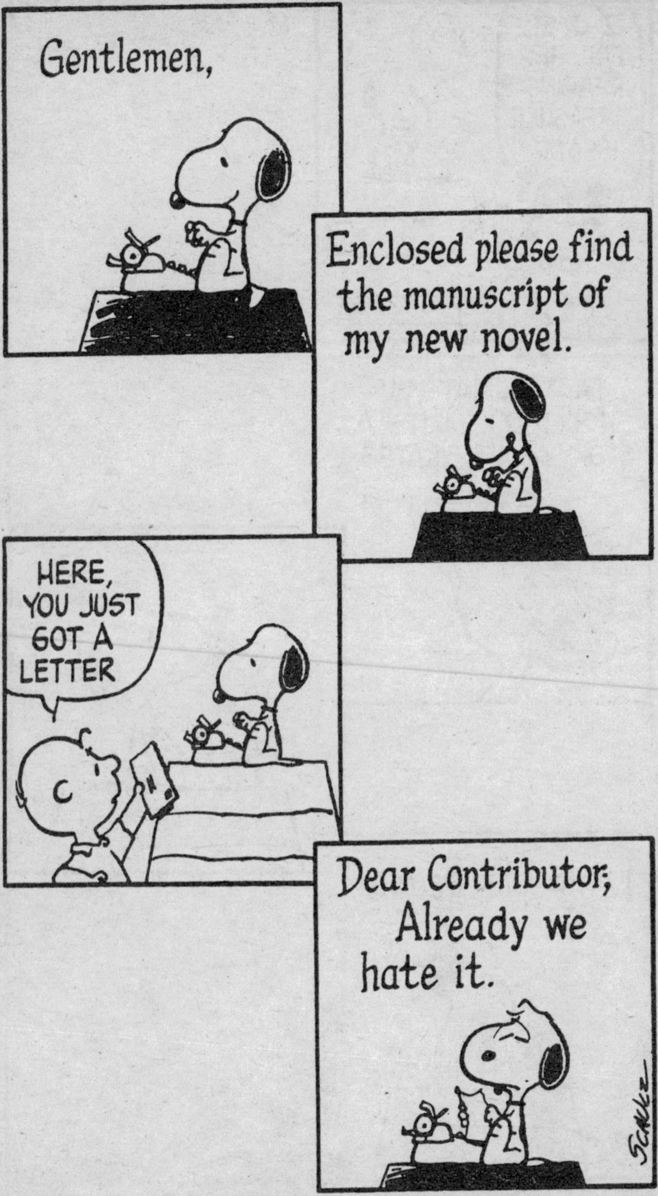
Gentlemen,
Enclosed please find the manuscript of my new novel.
HERE, YOU JUST GOT A LETTER
Dear Contributor;
Already we hate it.
SCHULZ

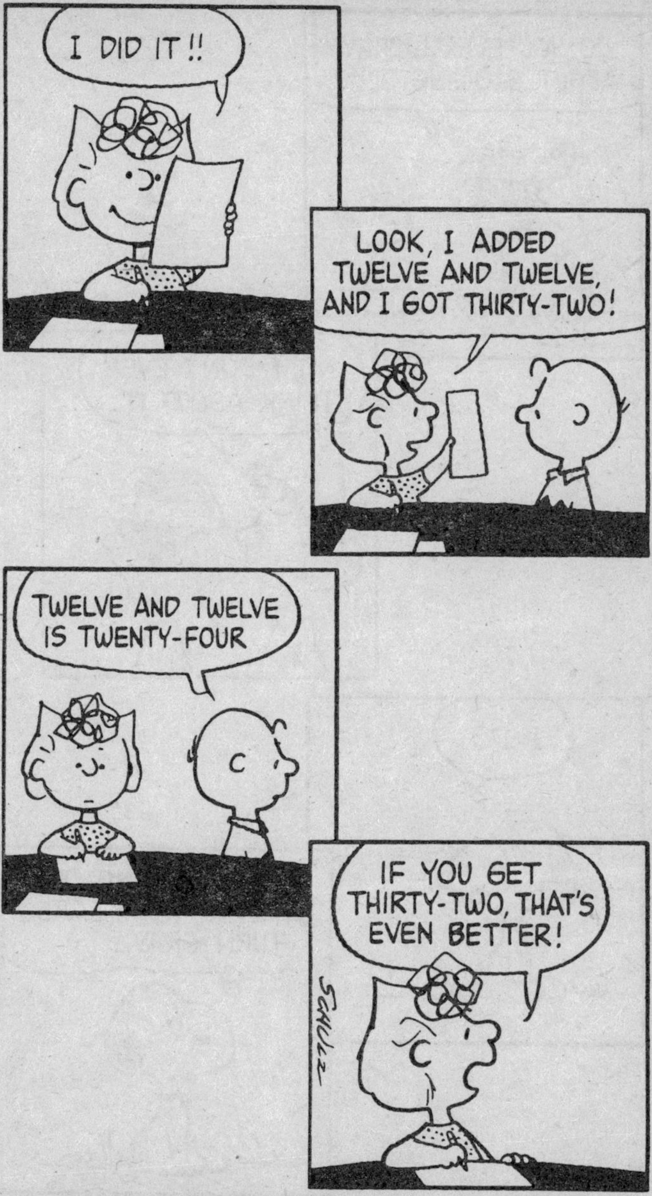
I DID IT!!
LOOK, I ADDED TWELVE AND TWELVE, AND I GOT THIRTY-TWO!
TWELVE AND TWELVE IS TWENTY-FOUR
IF YOU GET THIRTY-TWO, THAT'S EVEN BETTER!
SCHULZ

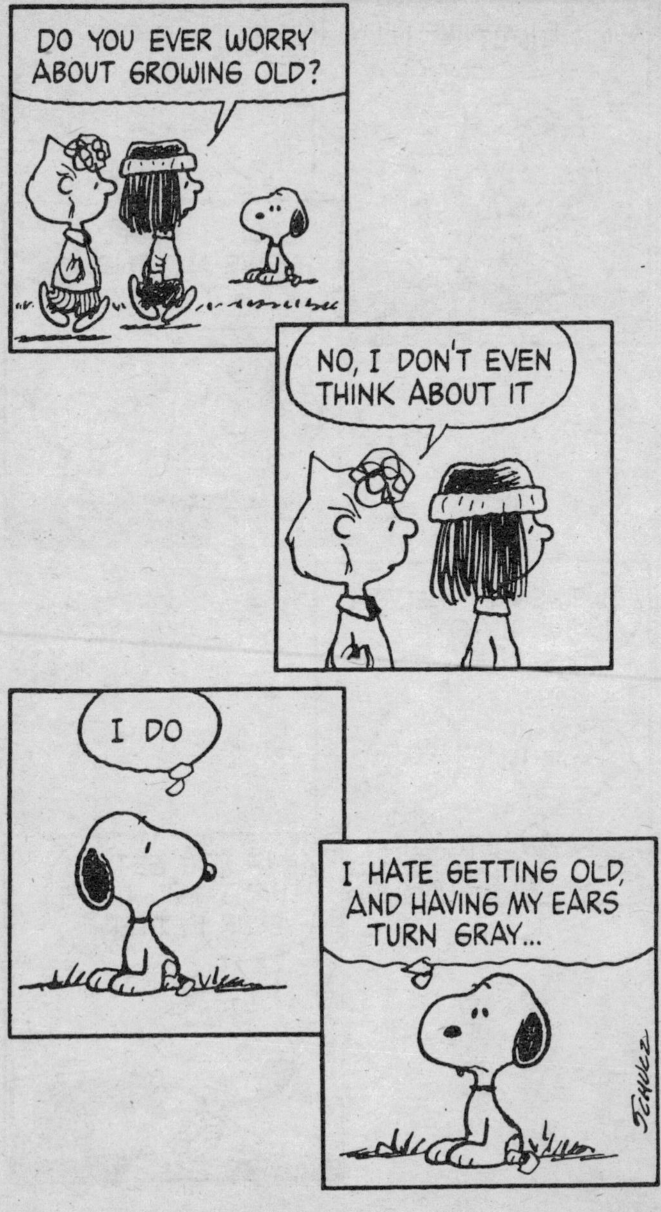
DO YOU EVER WORRY ABOUT GROWING OLD?
NO, I DON'T EVEN THINK ABOUT IT
I DO
I HATE GETTING OLD, AND HAVING MY EARS TURN GRAY...
SCHULZ

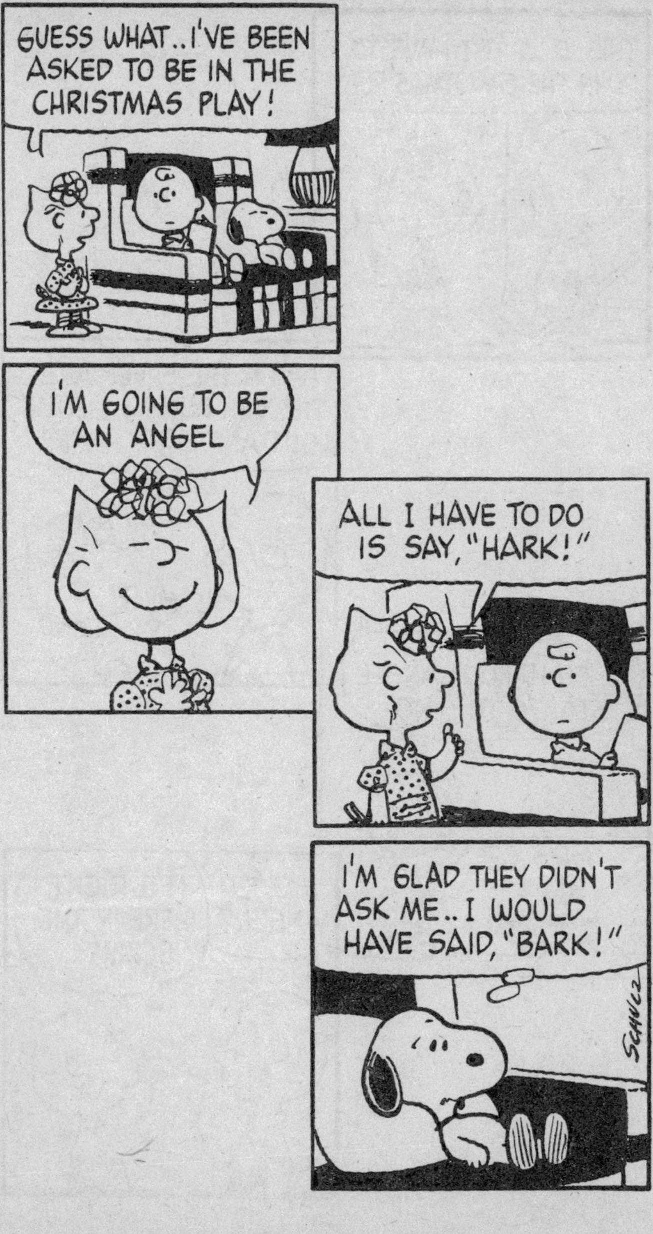
GUESS WHAT..I'VE BEEN ASKED TO BE IN THE CHRISTMAS PLAY!
I'M GOING TO BE AN ANGEL
ALL I HAVE TO DO IS SAY, "HARK!"
I'M GLAD THEY DIDN'T ASK ME..I WOULD HAVE SAID, "BARK!"
SCHULZ

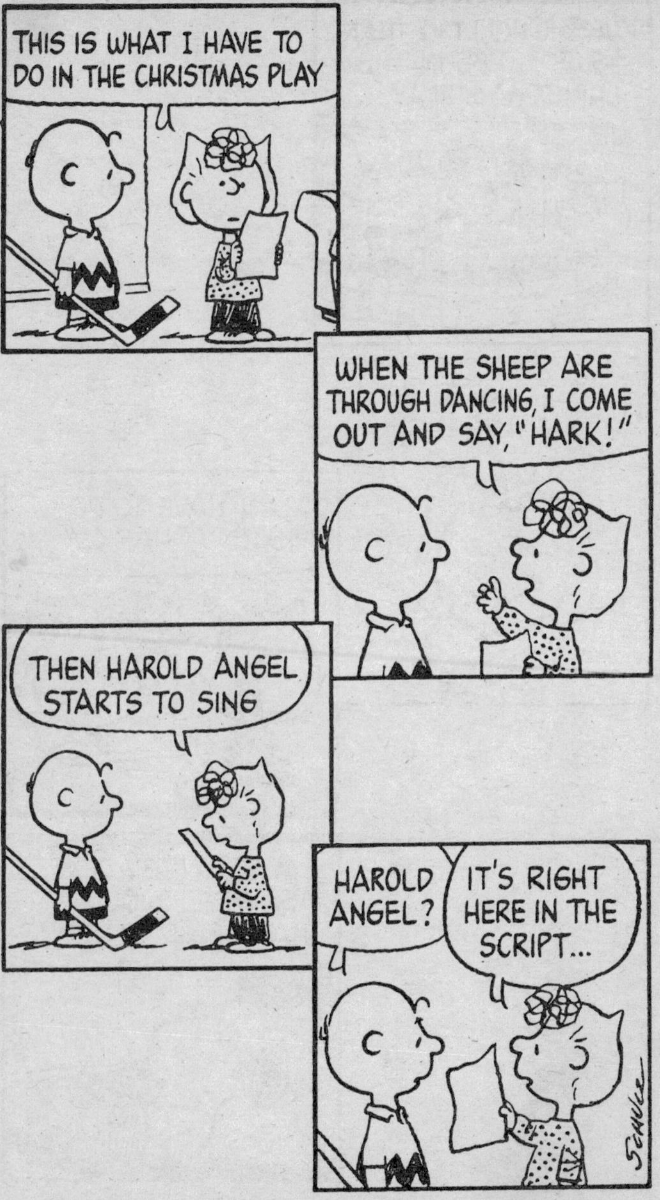
THIS IS WHAT I HAVE TO DO IN THE CHRISTMAS PLAY
WHEN THE SHEEP ARE THROUGH DANCING, I COME OUT AND SAY, "HARK!"
THEN HAROLD ANGEL STARTS TO SING
HAROLD ANGEL?
IT'S RIGHT HERE IN THE SCRIPT...
SCHULZ

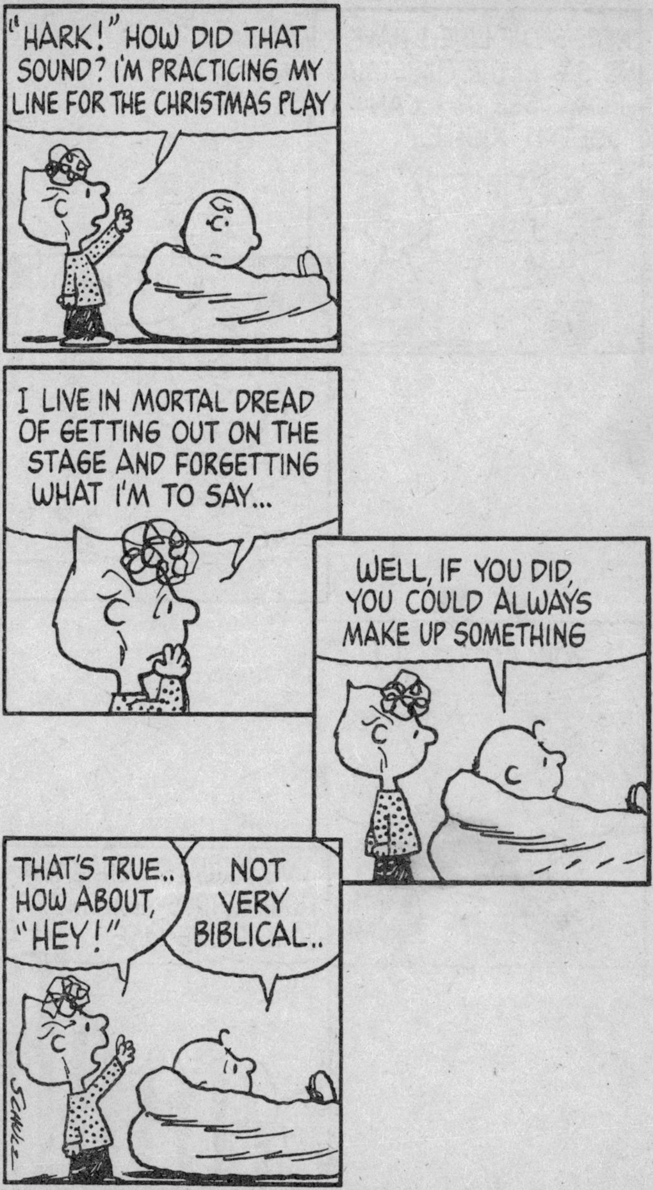
"HARK!" HOW DID THAT SOUND? I'M PRACTICING MY LINE FOR THE CHRISTMAS PLAY
I LIVE IN MORTAL DREAD OF GETTING OUT ON THE STAGE AND FORGETTING WHAT I'M TO SAY...
WELL, IF YOU DID, YOU COULD ALWAYS MAKE UP SOMETHING
THAT'S TRUE.. HOW ABOUT, "HEY!"
NOT VERY BIBLICAL..
SCHULZ

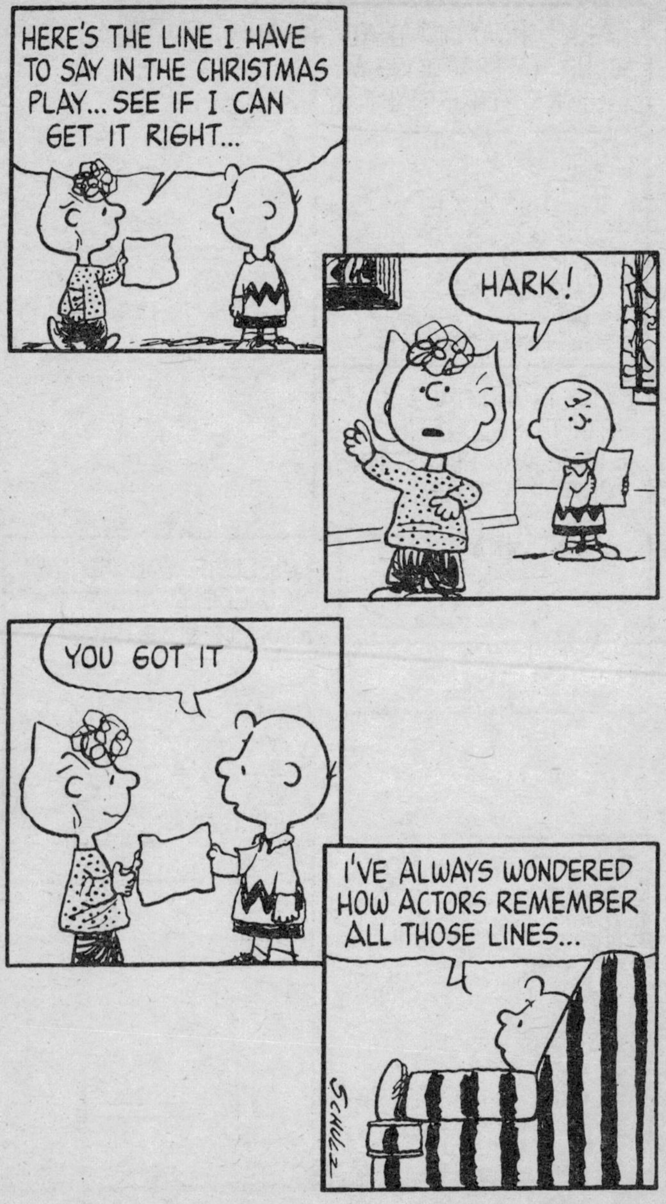
HERE'S THE LINE I HAVE TO SAY IN THE CHRISTMAS PLAY... SEE IF I CAN GET IT RIGHT...
HARK!
YOU GOT IT
I'VE ALWAYS WONDERED HOW ACTORS REMEMBER ALL THOSE LINES...
SCHULZ

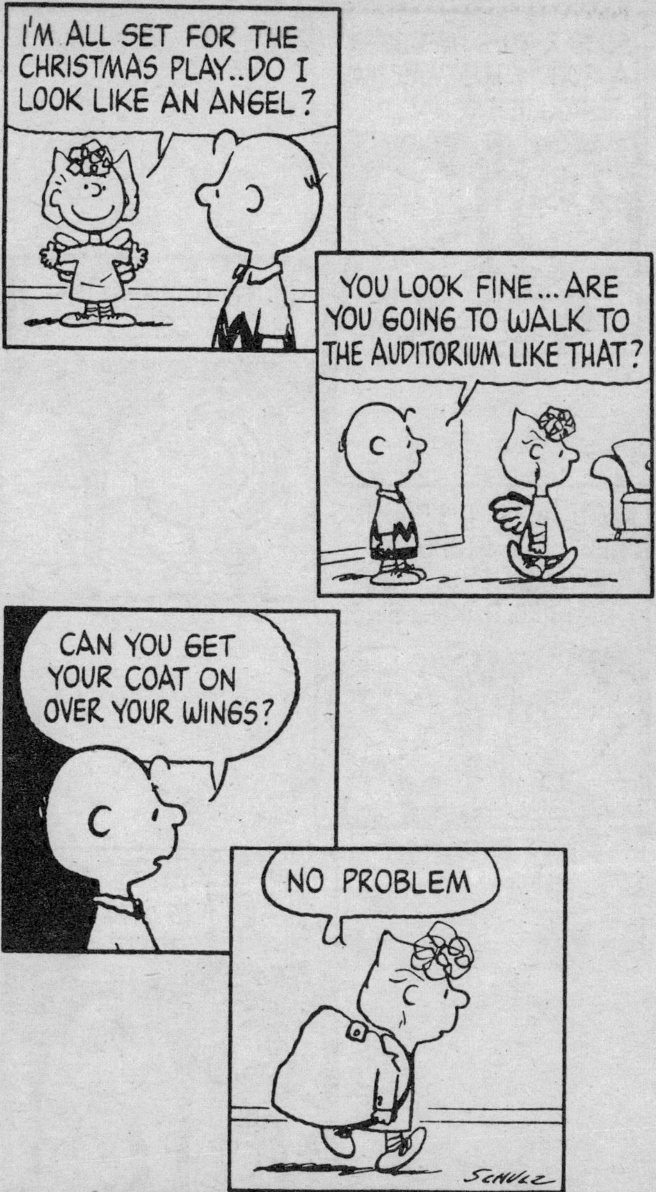
I'M ALL SET FOR THE CHRISTMAS PLAY..DO I LOOK LIKE AN ANGEL?
YOU LOOK FINE...ARE YOU GOING TO WALK TO THE AUDITORIUM LIKE THAT?
CAN YOU GET YOUR COAT ON OVER YOUR WINGS?
NO PROBLEM
SCHULZ

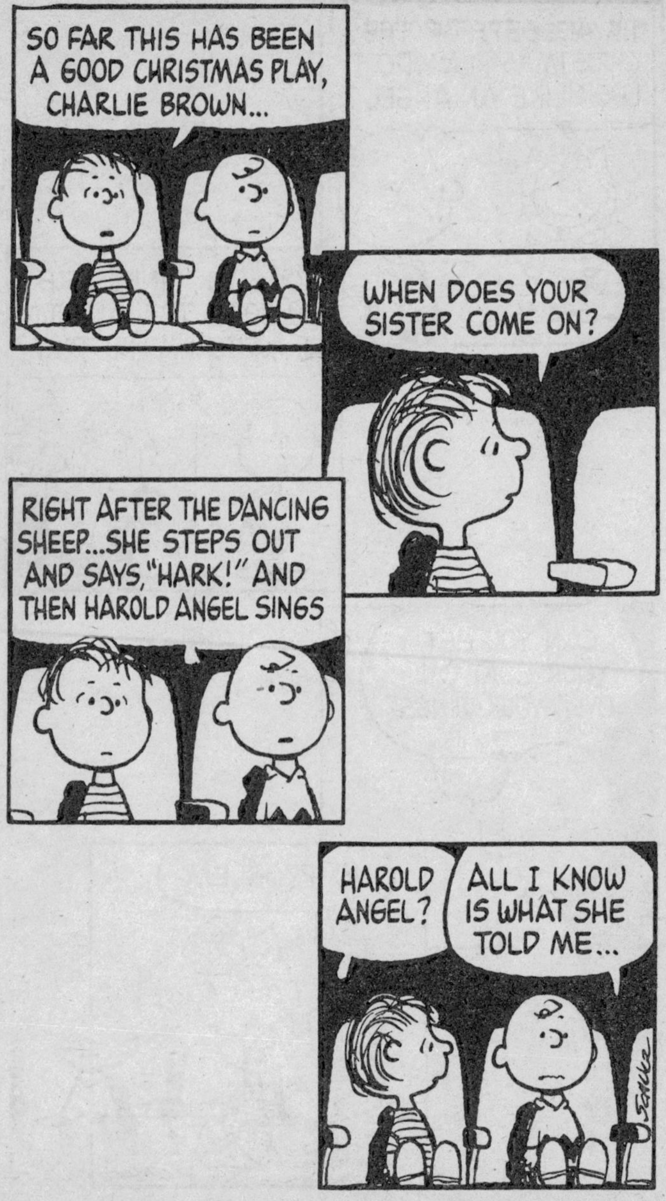
SO FAR THIS HAS BEEN A GOOD CHRISTMAS PLAY, CHARLIE BROWN...
WHEN DOES YOUR SISTER COME ON?
RIGHT AFTER THE DANCING SHEEP...SHE STEPS OUT AND SAYS, "HARK!" AND THEN HAROLD ANGEL SINGS
HAROLD ANGEL?
ALL I KNOW IS WHAT SHE TOLD ME...
SCHULZ

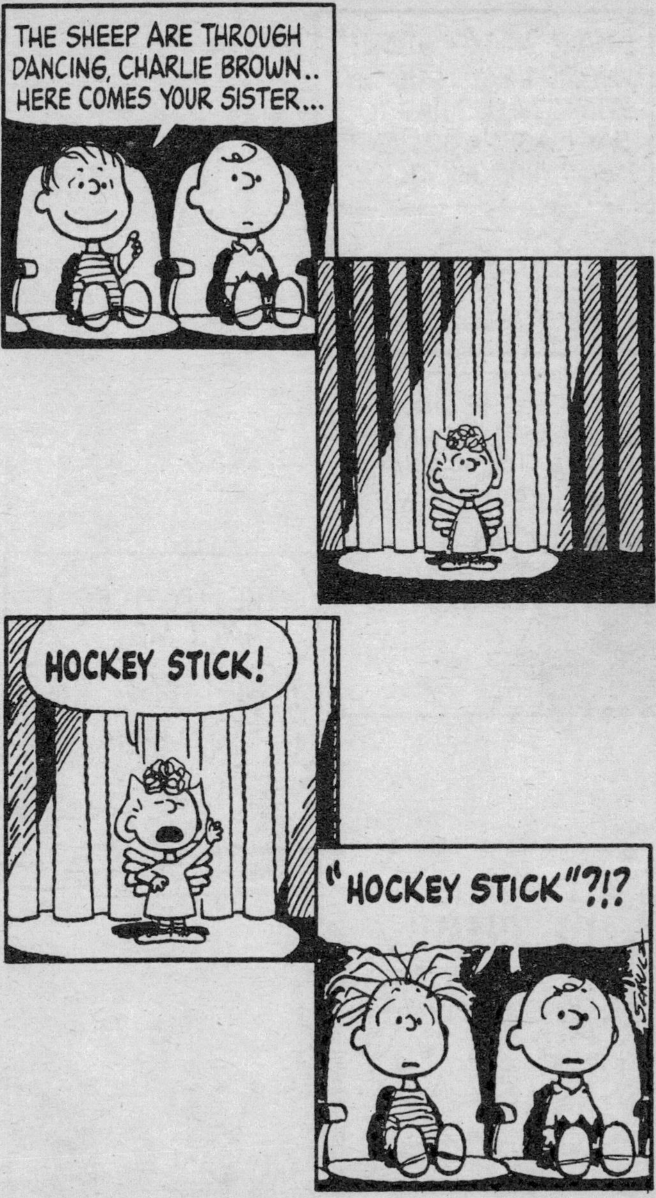
THE SHEEP ARE THROUGH DANCING, CHARLIE BROWN.. HERE COMES YOUR SISTER...
HOCKEY STICK!
"HOCKEY STICK"?!?
SCHULZ

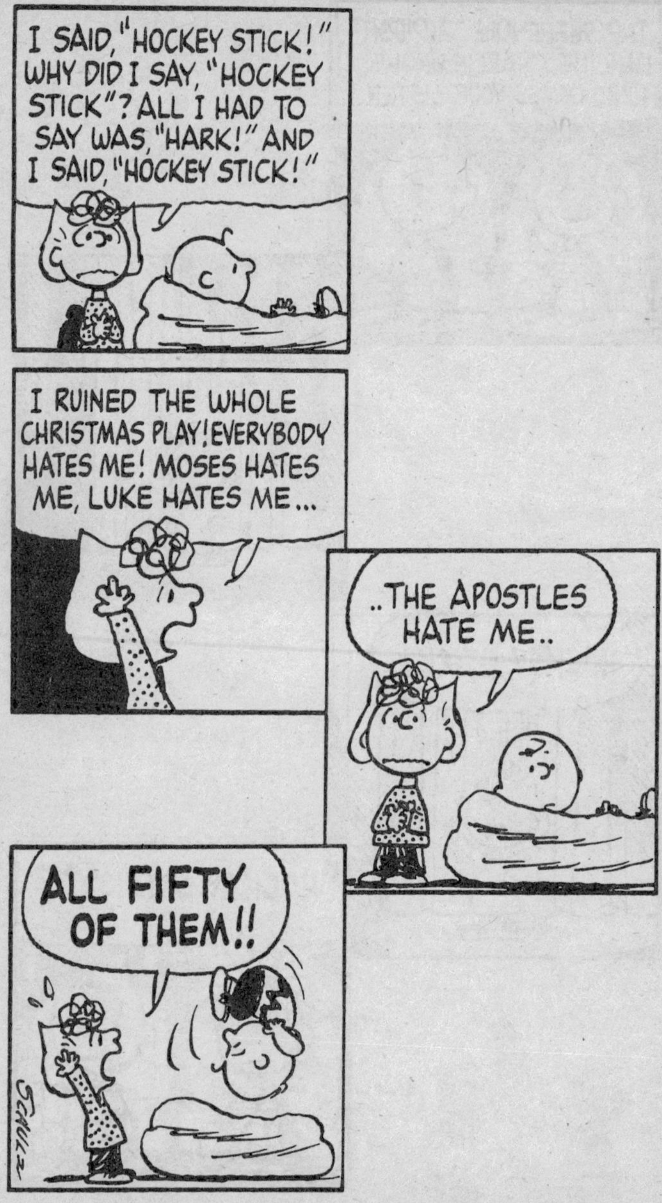
I SAID, "HOCKEY STICK!" WHY DID I SAY, "HOCKEY STICK"? ALL I HAD TO SAY WAS, "HARK!" AND I SAID, "HOCKEY STICK!"
I RUINED THE WHOLE CHRISTMAS PLAY! EVERYBODY HATES ME! MOSES HATES ME, LUKE HATES ME...
..THE APOSTLES HATE ME..
ALL FIFTY OF THEM!!
SCHULZ

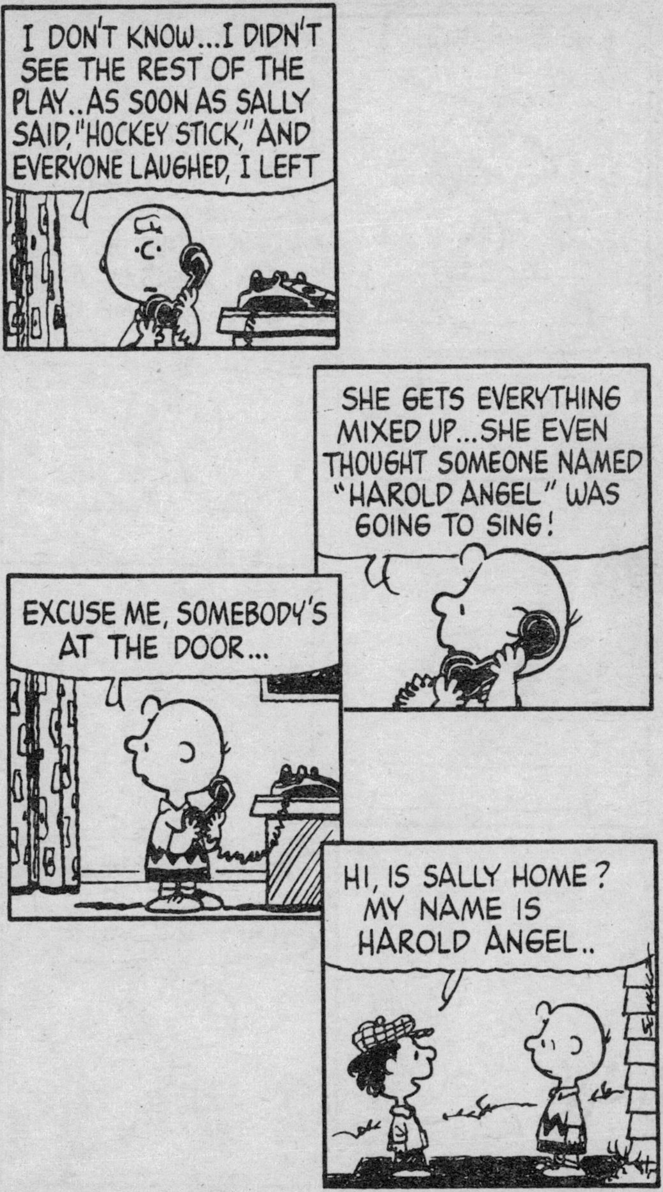
I DON'T KNOW...I DIDN'T SEE THE REST OF THE PLAY..AS SOON AS SALLY SAID, "HOCKEY STICK," AND EVERYONE LAUGHED, I LEFT
SHE GETS EVERYTHING MIXED UP...SHE EVEN THOUGHT SOMEONE NAMED "HAROLD ANGEL" WAS GOING TO SING!
EXCUSE ME, SOMEBODY'S AT THE DOOR...
HI, IS SALLY HOME? MY NAME IS HAROLD ANGEL..

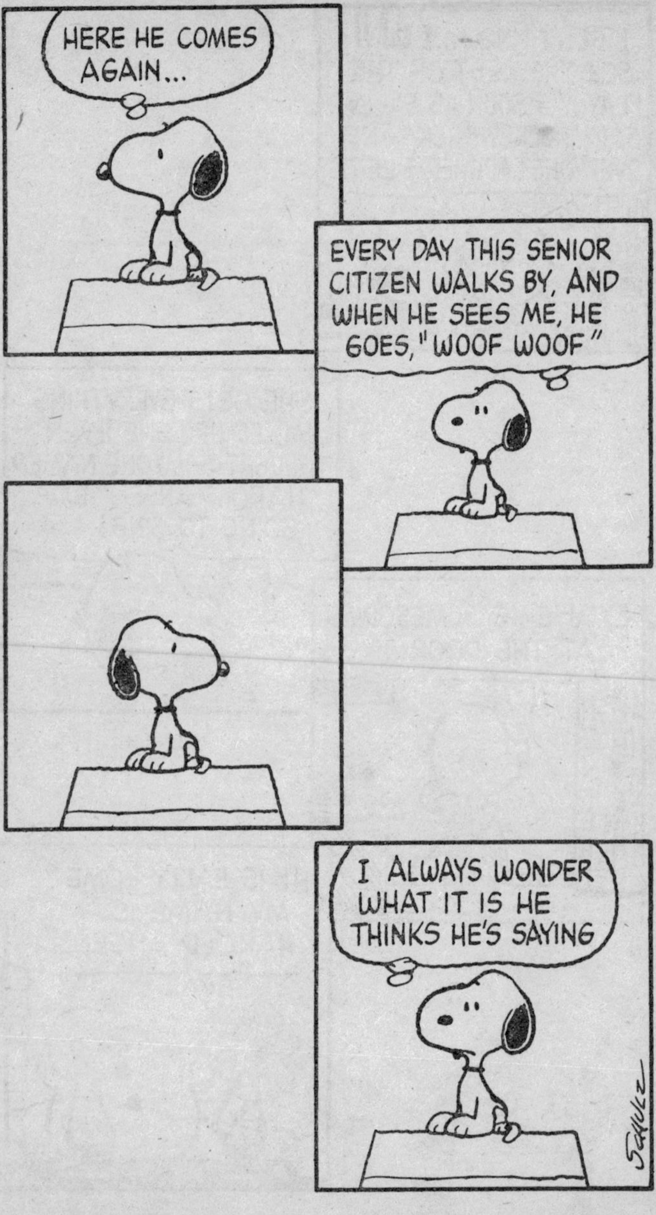
HERE HE COMES AGAIN...
EVERY DAY THIS SENIOR CITIZEN WALKS BY, AND WHEN HE SEES ME, HE GOES, "WOOF WOOF"
I ALWAYS WONDER WHAT IT IS HE THINKS HE'S SAYING

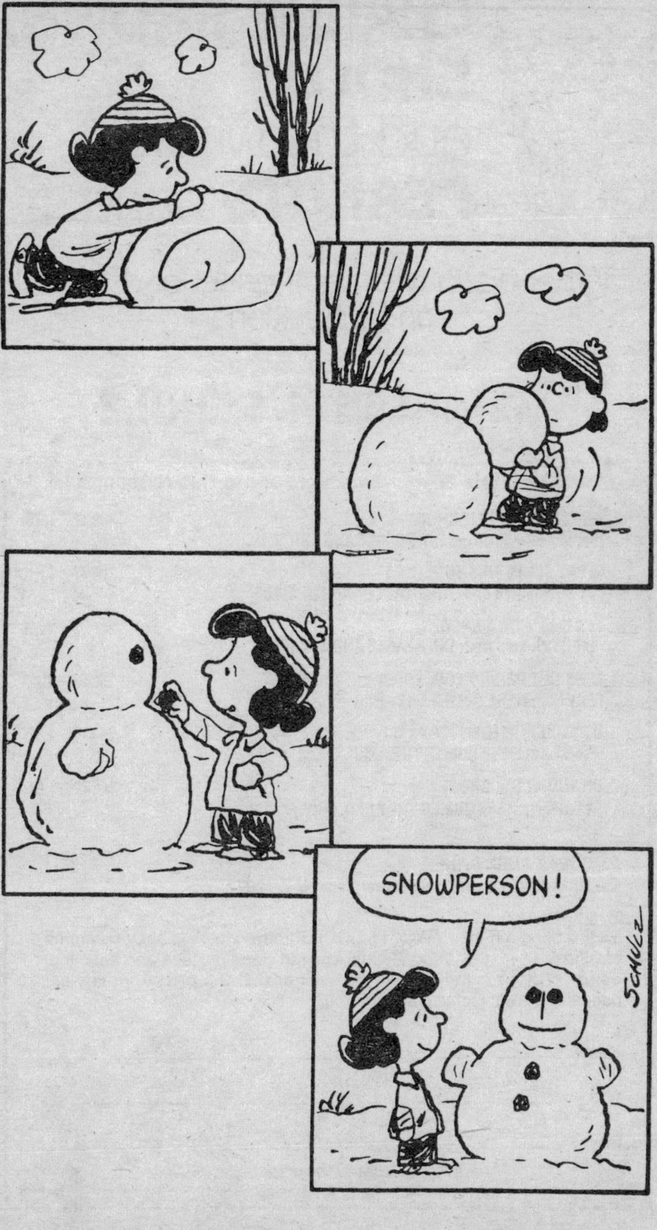
SNOWPERSON!
SCHULZ

CHARLIE BROWN, SNOOPY
and the whole
PEANUTS® gang...

Copr. © 1952 United Feature Syndicate, Inc.

together again with another set of daily trials and tribulations

by

CHARLES M. SCHULZ